THE Diabetic COOKBOOK

GRAND
AVENUE
BOOKS

Grand Avenue Books
An imprint of Meredith® Corporation

The Diabetic Cookbook
Contributing Editors: Sharyl Heiken, Rosemary Hutchinson
   (Spectrum Communication Services)
Senior Associate Art Director: Ken Carlson
Copy and Production Editor: Victoria Forlini
Contributing Designer: Mary Pat Crowley
Copy Chief: Terri Fredrickson
Editorial Operations Manager: Karen Schirm
Manager, Book Production: Rick von Holdt
Contributing Proofreaders: Maria Duryee, Sara Henderson
Electronic Production Coordinator: Paula Forest
Editorial and Design Assistants: Kaye Chabot, Mary Lee Gavin,
   Patricia Loder

Grand Avenue Books
Editor In Chief: Linda Raglan Cunningham
Design Director: Matt Strelecki
Executive Editor, Grand Avenue Books: Dan Rosenberg

Publisher: James D. Blume
Executive Director, Marketing: Jeffrey Myers
Executive Director, New Business Development: Todd M. Davis
Executive Director, Sales: Ken Zagor
Director, Operations: George A. Susral
Director, Production: Douglas M. Johnston
Business Director: Jim Leonard

Vice President and General Manager: Douglas J. Guendel

Meredith Publishing Group
President, Publishing Group: Stephen M. Lacy
Vice President-Publishing Director: Bob Mate

Meredith Corporation
Chairman and Chief Executive Officer: William T. Kerr

Chairman of the Executive Committee: E.T. Meredith III

All of us at Grand Avenue Books are dedicated to providing you with the information you need to create delicious foods. If for any reason you are not satisfied with this book, or if you have other comments, write to us at: Grand Avenue Books, Editorial Department LN-116, 1716 Locust Street, Des Moines, IA 50309-3023

Pictured on front cover: Oregano Chicken and Vegetables (see recipe, page 71)

THE Diabetic COOKBOOK

FROM HOMEY FAVORITES TO INNOVATIVE NEW DISHES, YOU'LL FIND FAMILY-PLEASING IDEAS HERE TO ADD VARIETY TO A DIABETIC MEAL PLAN.

Managing diabetes effectively involves balancing medication and proper diet with the right amount of physical activity. At first thought, the task of finding that balance might seem overwhelming. But with the help of a doctor, a registered dietitian, and handy references such as *The Diabetic Cookbook,* you can settle into a workable routine with a healthful meal and activity plan that works day in and day out.

The Diabetic Cookbook is an eye-catching, all-in-one volume that features captivating recipes as well as helpful facts to help manage diabetes. In addition, there are Exchange Lists for Meal Planning, based on a system developed by the American Diabetes Association and The American Dietetic Association.

The more than 125 luscious recipes in *The Diabetic Cookbook* were developed to meet the unique needs of people with diabetes, yet please anyone. That means you can cook everything from appetizers to main dishes to desserts for the whole family.

When diabetes is a fact of life for you, *The Diabetic Cookbook* will make coping with it easier. And it will make it a pleasure to plan and prepare delicious meals that both you and your family will enjoy.

Chicken with Peach Salsa **page 63**

CONTENTS

FOLLOWING A
Diabetic Diet

IF YOU HAVE DIABETES (OR COOK FOR SOMEONE WHO DOES), THE POINTERS YOU'LL FIND HERE WILL HELP YOU PLAN AND STICK TO A GREAT-TASTING, EVERYDAY MEAL PLAN THAT'S DESIGNED TO MANAGE DIABETES AND PROMOTE GOOD HEALTH.

Treating diabetes successfully is a balancing act. You need to rely on the skill and knowledge of the professionals on your health-care team, but you also must take an active roll in monitoring your eating patterns and adjusting your lifestyle so you can be healthy and productive. To help you get started, these next few pages are filled with the basics—a brief rundown of what diabetes is, how it's treated, and, most importantly, how to enjoy meals in spite of the illness. You'll learn how to use food to manage your blood sugar levels and how to build a meal plan using the Exchange Lists for Meal Planning from the American Diabetes Association and the American Dietetic Association. What's more, you'll find nutrition advice, tips for shopping, cooking hints, and suggestions for eating out. Best of all, the recipes in this book are delectable dishes that both you and your family will enjoy.

Diabetes: What Is It?

To understand diabetes, you need to know how it affects your body. When your body is working normally, it takes the food you eat and turns it into glucose (blood sugar), and then uses the glucose for energy. To move the glucose from your blood stream into your body's cells, the pancreas produces the hormone insulin. In people who have diabetes, however, this glucose-shuttling system breaks down because either the pancreas doesn't produce enough insulin or the body can't use the insulin it does produce. This causes high levels of glucose to accumulate in the blood stream. There are two types of diabetes: type 1 and type 2. The treatment that's best for you depends on the type you have.

Type 1 Diabetes

In type 1 diabetes, the body's immune system destroys the insulin-producing cells in the pancreas, which means the pancreas produces no insulin. When untreated, type 1 diabetes results in dangerously high glucose levels in the blood, which can lead to coma or death. The treatment of type 1 diabetes usually involves taking daily insulin shots or using an insulin pump (which automatically dispenses insulin) to keep blood glucose levels within normal range.

Type 1 diabetes most often appears during childhood or during the young-adult years, and until recently was referred to as insulin-dependent

or juvenile diabetes. Type 1 diabetes may come on suddenly, and someone with the illness may have the following symptoms:

- high blood glucose levels
- high levels of sugar in the urine
- frequent urination
- intense hunger or thirst
- rapid or unexplained weight loss
- weakness and fatigue
- mood swings and irritability
- nausea and vomiting

Type 2 Diabetes

People with type 2 diabetes have a pancreas that produces some insulin, but their cells resist insulin's message to let in blood glucose. This condition, known as insulin resistance, results in high levels of glucose in the blood stream. Type 2 diabetes has mild symptoms and usually develops gradually. Overweight adults are the most susceptible to type 2 diabetes, although there is a rising occurrence of the illness in overweight children. In the past, this type of diabetes was called non-insulin dependent or adult-onset diabetes. The typical symptoms include:

- increased thirst and frequent urination
- moodiness and fatigue
- nausea
- increased appetite
- unexplained weight loss
- frequent hard-to-heal infections, often affecting the skin, gums, vaginal area, or bladder
- vision problems, especially blurring
- tingling or numbness in the hands or feet
- dry, itchy skin

Controlling Diabetes Successfully

Keeping blood glucose levels within normal ranges is the key to controlling diabetes. When your blood glucose levels are in check, you'll feel better and avoid or delay complications. Start your treatment by turning to a physician who will help you assemble a health-care team. These professionals will help you to develop a healthful diet plan, a safe level of physical activity, and, if necessary, a medication regimen—all customized to your lifestyle and type of diabetes. Here are some general guidelines for treating diabetes:

Type 1 Diabetes: Because people with type 1 diabetes have a pancreas that produces no insulin, controlling blood glucose levels can be challenging. A typical treatment plan includes periodic blood sugar monitoring throughout the day, insulin injections, controlled regular physical activity, and a carefully planned diet with three meals and two snacks that often are matched to the times the insulin is at its highest level.

Type 2 Diabetes: Often type 2 diabetes can be treated without medication, relying on a customized meal plan and regular physical activity. In more severe cases, home blood glucose monitoring and oral medication or insulin are part of the treatment. Because people with newly diagnosed type 2 diabetes are often overweight, the meal plan usually is designed to promote weight loss.

Flexible Strategies for Meal Planning

Eating healthfully is one of the most important steps you can take to control diabetes. But this doesn't have to mean a strict diet with little room to accommodate your food likes or dislikes. Although you may have heard that diabetic diets are rigid, health-care professionals today generally agree that diets with no flexibility don't work.

To develop your meal plan, your doctor will most likely refer you to a registered dietitian who will work with you to customize a plan. (To obtain a referral for a dietitian, call The American Dietetic Association at 800/366-1655 or phone the American Diabetes Association at 800/342-2383.) The plan will take into account the type of diabetes medication you are taking, whether you need to lose weight, and if you

Keeping Tabs on Blood Glucose

If you are taking insulin shots or are on oral medication, monitoring your blood glucose level is important. Your health-care practitioner probably will advise you to test your blood sugar level before each meal with a finger-prick test. Your doctor also will give you some guidelines for adjusting your food consumption, physical activity, or medication when the readings are too high or too low. A normal blood glucose level before eating is 70 to 110 mg/dl. Your doctor will work with you to determine what range is best for you.

have other health problems (such as heart disease or high blood pressure). To work best, the meal plan should fit your lifestyle and include many of your favorite foods. You shouldn't need to rely on special "diabetic" foods.

The guidelines you'll follow are the same ones recommended for anyone who wants to maintain a healthful diet. Your diet should:

- Allow you to achieve and maintain a healthful weight. If you are overweight, losing 10 or 20 pounds can help you better control your blood glucose levels, lower your blood cholesterol, and achieve a blood pressure that is normal for your age. For those on insulin or oral diabetes medication, losing weight may allow you to take less medication.

- Include many different foods. Because you need more than 40 different nutrients for good health, it's important that you eat a variety of foods. Besides, eating the same foods over and over is boring!

- Emphasize grains, vegetables, and fruits. These foods are good sources of vitamins, minerals, and fiber. What's more, they can help reduce the risk of heart disease and cancer when you include them in a low-fat diet.

- Help reduce the risk of heart disease—that is your diet should be low in fat, especially saturated fat, and cholesterol. Health experts say a healthful diet should average no more than 30 percent of total daily calories from fat, less than 10 percent of calories from saturated fat,

and no more than 300 milligrams of cholesterol. This rule is especially important for those who have diabetes and thus have a greater risk of heart disease.

- Keep salt and sodium in check. Too much sodium (one of the components of salt) increases the risk of high blood pressure in some people. A limit of about 2,400 mg of sodium per day is generally recommended. Your dietitian will tell you what daily sodium level is best for you.

- Be moderate in sugar. Yes, sugar can be part of your healthful meal plan! In the past, diabetic patients often were told to avoid table sugar (sucrose) because this simple carbohydrate was thought to cause a greater rise in blood glucose than the complex carbohydrates, such as pasta, potatoes, or bread. But recent research has shown that simple carbohydrates don't raise blood glucose levels any higher or faster than other carbohydrates. As a result, the American Diabetes Association now says that you can include some sugar in your meal plan as long as you count it as part of your total carbohydrates for the day. Check with your dietitian for suggestions on how to occasionally include sugar in your meal plans.

Creating a Meal Plan

The goal of an individualized meal plan is to help you decide when, what, and how much to eat. By following the plan, you can feel comfortable that you're getting the vitamins, minerals, and fiber you need as well as limiting fat, cholesterol, and sodium. If your weight is within normal range for your height, the calories in your plan should be enough to help you stay at that weight. If you need to lose a few pounds, the plan should scale back the calories so you can lose weight gradually.

A healthful diabetic meal plan also will regulate the number of calories from carbohydrates, fat, and protein you eat daily. The calories from these nutrients will affect your blood glucose level. However, carbohydrates have the greatest effect. Generally, carbohydrates (4 calories per gram) should make up 50% to 60% of the calories in your diet, while fat (9 calories per gram) should be less than 30% and protein (4 calories per gram) should range between 10% and 20%.

Your registered dietitian may talk with you about using the Exchange Lists for Meal Planning, a system designed by the American Diabetes Association and the American Dietetic Association. If you decide to use the exchange system, your dietitian will help you customize a "pattern" of exchanges to use.

Exchange Primer

Whether you're new to the system or have been using it for a while, these hints will give you a quick rundown of the fundamentals of food exchanges. Exchanges are divided into the following categories of foods:

- the Carbohydrates Group, which includes starches, fruits, milk, other carbohydrates, and vegetables.
- the Meat and Meat Substitutes Group (protein), which contains very lean, lean, medium-fat, and high-fat lists.
- the Fat Group, which includes lists that classify fats as monounsaturated, polyunsaturated, and saturated.

Each list features foods that are roughly equivalent in number of calories and amount of carbohydrates, protein, and fat. One serving of a food is called an "exchange" because you can substitute it for a serving of any other food on that list. For example, from the fruit list, you can replace $3/4$ cup of canned mandarin oranges with a small apple or half of a small mango. The purpose of the lists is to give you as many choices as possible and add variety to your meals.

In addition, there is a list of free foods, which shows items that contain few calories and can be

included in small amounts, as well as a list of combination foods, which helps you fit dishes composed of more than one type of food exchange into your meal plan.

To understand each of the exchange lists better, refer to these general serving size suggestions and helpful exchange tips. (Also, see the detailed Exchange Lists on pages 280 to 287.)

Starch List

The starch list includes breads, cereals, grains, pasta, starchy vegetables, crackers, snacks, and cooked dried beans, peas, and lentils. One serving contains about 80 calories, 15 grams of carbohydrate, 3 grams of protein, and 0 to 1 gram of fat.

One starch exchange can be:
- 1 ounce of a bread product, such as 1 slice of bread or $1/2$ of a small bagel
- $1/2$ cup of cooked cereal, grain, pasta, or starchy vegetable, such as peas
- $3/4$ to 1 ounce of most snack foods
Include at least 6 exchanges daily from the starch list in your meal plan.

Starch Exchange Tips
- Rely on foods from the starchy list for B vitamins and iron. Whole grains and beans, peas, and lentils also contain a rich amount of fiber.
- If possible, avoid adding fat to items from the starch list.
- If you do make a starch vegetable (such as corn, potatoes, or peas) with fat, count one serving as 1 starch exchange and 1 fat exchange.
- Refer to the "Starchy Foods Prepared with Fat" section of the starch list (see page 281) when you're planning to include foods such as French fries, microwave popcorn, and muffins in your meal plan. A serving of each of these counts as 1 starch exchange and 1 fat exchange.
- Look on the meat and meat substitutes list for beans, peas, and lentils. One serving counts as 1 starch exchange and 1 very lean meat exchange.

Consistency Is the Key
Keeping your blood glucose level steady will make managing your diabetes easier. Here's what you can do to help keep the level constant.
- Eat meals and snacks at about the same time each day.
- Eat about the same amount of food each day.
- Don't skip meals or snacks.

Fruit List

In addition to great flavor, fruits provide a double nutritional bonus—they're generally low in fat and excellent sources of vitamin A, vitamin C, and potassium. Fruits, along with grains and vegetables, also contain phytochemicals—plant compounds that are believed to play a roll in preventing heart disease and cancer.

One fruit exchange supplies about 60 calories and 15 grams of carbohydrate. Fruit exchanges include listings for fresh, frozen, canned, and dried fruits, as well as fruit juices.

One fruit exchange can be:

- 1 small to medium piece of fresh fruit, such as an apple or orange
- 1/2 cup of canned or fresh fruit or fruit juice
- 1/4 cup of dried fruit

For good health, eat 2 to 4 exchanges daily from the fruit list.

Fruit Exchange Tips

- Be sure to eat deep yellow or orange fruits (cantaloupe, apricots, peaches, or mangoes) and "high C" options (oranges, grapefruits, strawberries, or kiwi fruits) frequently.
- Canned fruit exchanges are based on products labeled "no added sugar" or those packed in juice or in extra-light syrup. Each has about the same amount of carbohydrates per serving.
- Serving sizes for canned fruit include the fruit and a small amount of juice.
- 1/2 cup of cranberries or rhubarb sweetened with sugar substitute can be included in a meal plan as a free food.
- Eating whole fruit will provide more fiber than drinking fruit juice does.

Milk List

Dairy products, such as milk and yogurt, provide a rich supply of calcium, the nutrient that helps build strong bones. Milk products also provide protein, phosphorous, magnesium, and vitamins A, D, and B-12, as well as riboflavin.

Because the fat and calorie content of milk products varies, the exchanges on this list are divided into:

- Fat-free/low-fat milk products: These products have 12 grams of carbohydrate, 8 grams of protein, and from 0 to 3 grams of fat. They are about 90 calories per serving.
- Reduced-fat milk products: These products have 12 grams of carbohydrate, 8 grams of protein, and 5 grams of fat. They are about 120 calories per serving.
- Whole milk products: These products have 12 grams of carbohydrate, 8 grams of protein, and 8 grams of fat. They are about 150 calories per serving.

Keeping Track of Carbohydrates

In addition to the exchange system, another way for people with diabetes to monitor the foods they eat is to count carbohydrates. Based on the fact that carbohydrates have a significant affect on glucose levels in the blood, this technique involves simply counting the grams of carbohydrate you eat each day.

To use this method, ask your registered dietitian to develop a meal plan that shows you how many grams of carbohydrate you can eat at each meal or snack. Armed with this information, you can choose foods that total the specified number of carbohydrates allowed.

Here's how to find out how many carbohydrates are in foods. For the recipes in this book, look under Nutrition Facts for the number of grams in each serving. For other foods, look on the exchange lists on pages 280 to 287. And, on some commercial food product labels, you'll find that the "nutrition facts" panels list the grams of carbohydrate in a serving. For even more information, check a bookstore for references that list carbohydrate counts for common foods.

Because it allows a greater range of food choices, many diabetics say carbohydrate counting is simpler to use than the exchange system. Some believe it allows better blood glucose control. However, for the technique to work, you must strictly monitor your blood glucose level, be accurate in measuring portion sizes, and stick to a well-balanced diet that has the appropriate number of calories and the right amount of fat. Discuss the pros and cons of carbohydrate counting with your dietitian.

LOW IN BOTH CALORIES AND FAT, ITEMS ON THE VEGETABLE EXCHANGE
LIST ARE NUTRITION BARGAINS. THEY ARE GOOD SOURCES OF VITAMIN A,
VITAMIN C, FOLIC ACID, IRON, MAGNESIUM, AND FIBER.

One milk exchange can be:

- 1 cup of milk (all types)
- ³/₄ cup of plain yogurt or 1 cup of yogurt sweetened with sugar substitute.

   Eat or drink 2 to 3 exchanges daily from the milk list.

Milk Exchange Tips

- Select items from the fat-free/low-fat milk group most often.
- Many items you may think of as "milk" are on other lists.
  - Look for cheeses on the meat list.
  - You'll find cream, half-and-half, and cream cheese on the fat list.
  - Rice milk is on the starch list.
  - Soy milk is a medium-fat meat.
  - You'll find chocolate milk, low-fat yogurt with fruit, ice cream, and frozen yogurt on the other carbohydrates list.

Other Carbohydrates List

This list helps you occasionally fit sweets, such as cakes, cookies, ice cream, or pie, as well as higher-fat snacks, such as potato or tortilla chips, into your meal plan. One other carbohydrates exchange contains about 15 grams of carbohydrate.

Other Carbohydrates Exchange Tips

- Be moderate when you choose from this list. These foods are low in nutrients.
- To use a food from the other carbohydrates list, substitute it for a starch, fruit, or milk exchange.
- Remember the serving sizes for these foods are small because they contain added sugars or fat.
- Take note that some choices count as 1 or more carbohydrate and fat exchanges. Adjust your meal plan accordingly.

Vegetable List

Vegetables are a nutritional bargain because they're low in both calories and fat. They are good sources of vitamin A, vitamin C, folic acid, iron, magne-

sium, and fiber. One vegetable exchange contains about 5 grams of carbohydrate, 2 grams of protein, 1 to 4 grams of fiber, and 25 calories.

One vegetable exchange can be:

- 1 cup of raw vegetables, such as lettuce, spinach, or broccoli flowerets
- ¹/₂ cup of cooked vegetables or vegetable juice

   Plan on 3 to 5 vegetable exchanges daily.

Vegetable Exchange Tips

- Because vegetable exchanges are low in calories and carbohydrates, you can eat 1 or 2 exchanges at a meal or snack without counting them. If you eat 3 or more vegetable exchanges at a time, count them as 1 carbohydrate exchange (15 grams of carbohydrate).
- Remember to opt for dark green, leafy vegetables, such as spinach, romaine, broccoli, and cabbage, several times each week. Also be sure to eat several servings of deep yellow and orange varieties, such as carrots and red peppers (or, sweet potatoes and acorn squash from the starch list), each week.
- Vegetable exchanges high in vitamin C include tomatoes, Brussels sprouts, greens, sweet or hot peppers, broccoli, and cauliflower.

Meat and Meat Substitutes List

Meat, poultry, fish, eggs, cheese, peanut butter, and tofu are part of the meat and meat substitutes list, providing protein, B vitamins, iron, and zinc. Because the fat and calorie content of meat products vary, the exchange list is divided into very lean, lean, medium-fat, and high-fat categories.

- Very lean meat items have no carbohydrates, 7 grams of protein, and from 0 to 1 gram of fat. One exchange (1 ounce) has about 35 calories.
- Lean meat items have no carbohydrates, 7 grams of protein, and 3 grams of fat. One exchange (1 ounce) has about 55 calories.
- Medium-fat meat items have no carbohydrates, 7 grams of protein, and 5 grams of fat. One exchange (1 ounce) has about 75 calories.
- High-fat meat items have no carbohydrates, 7 grams of protein, and 8 grams of fat. One exchange (1 ounce) has about 100 calories.

One meat exchange can be:

- 1 ounce cooked meat, poultry, or fish
- 1 ounce cheese or 1 egg
- $1/2$ cup cooked dried beans, peas, or lentils
- 2 tablespoons peanut butter
- 3 slices bacon

Select 4 to 6 exchanges daily from the meat and meat substitutes list.

Meat Exchange Tips

- If the information you have (for example, the exchanges given for the recipes in this book) lists simply "meat" exchanges, you can determine if the exchanges are very lean, lean, medium fat, or high fat by looking up the type of meat, poultry, fish, or other protein on the Meat and Meat Substitutes List (page 284).
- To judge portion sizes use these guidelines: An ounce of cooked lean meat, poultry, or fish is about the size of a matchbook and 3 ounces is the size of a deck of cards. One ounce of cheese is about a 1-inch cube.

- A small chicken leg or thigh or $1/2$ cup cottage cheese or tuna equals 2 meat exchanges.
- A small hamburger, half of a whole chicken breast, a medium pork chop, or one unbreaded fish fillet equals 3 meat exchanges.
- Count a serving of dried beans, peas, or lentils as 1 very lean meat exchange and 1 starch exchange.
- Use selections from the high-fat meat list sparingly—three times per week at most.
- Two tablespoons of peanut butter or a hot dog count as 1 high-fat exchange. Note that smaller servings of peanut butter and bacon are counted as fat exchanges instead of meat exchanges.

Fat List

When it comes to including fats in your meal plan, be cautious. Small amounts can add up to a lot of calories and can add extra pounds quickly or keep you from losing weight. A high-fat diet, especially one high in saturated fat, increases your risk for heart disease and some cancers. Each fat exchange provides about 5 grams of fat and 45 calories.

One fat exchange can be:

- 1 teaspoon vegetable oil, regular margarine, butter, or mayonnaise
- 1 tablespoon regular salad dressing
- 10 peanuts, 6 almonds or cashews, or 4 pecan or walnut halves
- 2 teaspoons peanut butter
- 1 slice bacon

Exchange List Rules of the Road

- Cooked measures are used for serving sizes on the exchange lists.
- Accuracy counts when it comes to portion sizes. Underestimating portions can affect both your blood glucose and your weight. Pay attention to the serving sizes given in the exchange lists and on food labels. Weigh and measure your food until you can accurately judge portion sizes.
- Vary your choices from the food exchange list to ensure you get a variety of nutrients. Because exchanges from the starch, fruit, and milk lists contain about the same amount of carbohydrates, you may exchange choices from these groups. But remember you may be missing some nutrients. For example, if you often trade your milk exchange for starches or fruits, you may not get enough calcium.
- Beans, peas, lentils, bacon, and peanut butter are listed in two exchange lists so you have more flexibility when planning meals.

Sugar Alert

Too much sugar in your meal plan can throw your diabetic diet off track. Often food items contain sugar in forms that may surprise you. Below is a list of terms that tell you a product contains sugar in some form. When reading the ingredient listing on a package, be aware that the ingredients are listed in descending order by weight. A food may be high in sugar if one of these names is the first or second ingredient in the list or if several types appear in the listing.

- sugar (sucrose)
- brown sugar
- raw sugar
- invert sugar
- honey
- molasses
- fruit juice concentrate
- glucose (dextrose)
- lactose
- fructose
- maltose
- syrup
- corn syrup
- high-fructose corn syrup
- corn sweetener

Fat Exchange Tips

- Ask your dietitian how many fat exchanges you should include in your daily meal plan.
- Foods in the fat list are divided into monounsaturated, polyunsaturated, and saturated fats. Eating small amounts of monounsaturated and polyunsaturated fats may help fight heart disease, so choose these fats most often.
- Measure fat exchange foods carefully so the calories you consume don't get out of line.
- Avocados, olives, and coconut are on the fat list.
- Cream, half-and-half, and cream cheese also are on this list.
- Look for larger serving sizes of peanut butter and bacon on the high-fat meat exchanges list.
- You'll find the fat-free versions of margarine, salad dressing, mayonnaise, sour cream, and cream cheese on the free foods list.
- Nonstick cooking spray, nondairy creamers, and regular or light whipped topping also are on the free foods list.

Combination Foods List

Items such as casseroles, soups, pizza, and many of the recipes in this book are called combination or mixed foods because they include foods from two or more of the exchange lists.

You'll find exchanges for several types of mixed foods on the combination foods list on page 286.

For the recipes in this book, look under Nutrition Facts with each recipe for the food exchange listings. Many food manufacturers also list exchanges on their product labels. For other foods or your own recipes, you can estimate exchanges by determining what portion of an exchange each ingredient represents. For example, a serving of stew may contain 2 ounces of cooked lean beef (2 lean meat exchanges), $1/2$ cup of potato (1 starch exchange), and $1/2$ cup of carrots (1 vegetable exchange).

The Fast Foods List

To help you when you're eating out, this list includes values for many items commonly found at fast food restaurants. Because many of these foods are high in fat and calories, include them in your diet sparingly.

The Free Foods List

The free foods list includes items that contain less than 20 calories or less than 5 grams of carbohydrate per serving. You can enjoy as many as three

servings a day of the free foods listed with a serving size. But spread the servings throughout the day. Eating them all at once could affect your blood glucose level. You can enjoy as much as you like of the foods listed without a serving size.

Shopping Savvy

When you head to the supermarket, keep these health-conscious hints in mind. They will help you select the foods that are best for your meal plan—that is, ones that are low in calories, fat, and sodium, yet are high in vitamins, minerals, and fiber.

- Take the time to read labels. The "nutrition facts" panel on most labels will help you track what you eat. The panel lists amounts for fat, saturated fat, cholesterol, sodium, fiber, and other important nutrients as well as the number of calories and grams of carbohydrate, protein, and fat in each serving of the food. Use these numbers to calculate the exchanges in a serving of food. (Some food manufacturers list the exchanges on the package.) When it comes to fresh meat, poultry, seafood, vegetables, and fruits, supermarkets often show nutrition information on posters or have take-home brochures.
- Make "lean" your buzzword. Select low-fat cuts of meat labeled with the words "round" or "loin" in the name (for example, ground round or pork tenderloin). Opt for skinless poultry. Serve fish often, and go "vegetarian" every now and then, using dried beans, peas, and lentils.
- Choose fat-free and low-fat milk and yogurt rather than their whole milk counterparts.
- Try different types of reduced-fat cheese to find ones you like.
- Seek out low-fat snacks, such as pretzels, air-popped popcorn, flavored rice cakes, and baked bagel chips.
- Buy soft-style margarines with liquid vegetable oil as the first ingredient. Tub or liquid margarines are lower in saturated fat than stick margarine.

- Look for the fat-free or reduced-fat versions of sour cream, cream cheese, mayonnaise, salad dressing, and tartar sauce. Select a different brand each time you shop until you find the ones you like best.
- When buying frozen vegetables, opt for those without butter or sauces.
- Cut the sodium in your meals by using the reduced-sodium forms of Worcestershire sauce, soy sauce, broth or bouillon, canned beans, soups, luncheon meats, bacon, and ham.
- Boost fiber with whole-grain breads or crackers and high-fiber cereals.
- Buy tuna packed in water, not oil.
- Cook and bake with monounsaturated oils, such as olive, canola, or peanut oil.

Kitchen Essentials

Once you're ready to head to the kitchen, there are a number of things you can do to make the foods you eat more healthful. Here are a few.

- Bake, broil, grill, poach, steam, or microwave foods instead of frying.
- Use nonstick cooking spray, low-sodium broth, or fruit juice rather than oil or margarine to cook foods in a skillet.
- Trim all visible fat from meat and poultry.
- Substitute evaporated fat-free milk for whole milk or cream in sauces, soups, and baked goods.
- Skip the butter, margarine, or cooking oil called for in the package directions for rice or pasta.
- Replace one whole egg with two egg whites or $^{1}/_{4}$ cup egg substitute in recipes. This will help lower the cholesterol in the dish.
- Add fiber to baked goods by using whole wheat flour for up to half of the all-purpose flour called for in the recipe.
- Reduce the salt you use gradually. If you cut the salt in dishes a little at a time, you're less likely to notice the difference.
- Wash away some of the salt in canned vegetables by draining them in a colander, then rinsing with tap water.

Restaurant Round-Up

Eating out doesn't have to be your nutrition downfall. Here are some pointers to make eating in a restaurant fit into a diabetic lifestyle.

- Look for the baked, broiled, grilled, or steamed items on the menu rather than the fried ones.
- Seek out healthy choices. For example, choose rice rather than baked potatoes loaded with sour cream or butter and choose reduced- or low-calorie dressings for salads.
- Don't clean your plate. Restaurant portions are often gigantic. Eat only the amount you would at home and take the rest of your food home for another meal.
- Ask for salad dressings, sauces, and gravies on the side.
- Request that your food be prepared without added fat or salt.
- Skip the heavy sauces on chicken, fish, and vegetables. Instead, squeeze on a little lemon juice.
- Opt for diet drinks and use sugar substitutes.
- Forego rich desserts. Substitute a fruit cup or melon wedge instead.
- Use caution at fast food restaurants. Many provide brochures listing the nutrition information —and sometimes food exchanges—for their menu items. Ask for these.
- Minimize calories and fat by choosing fast food items such as grilled chicken sandwiches and small burgers.
- Enjoy French fries, but order the smallest size or split a larger size with a friend.

Get Physical

While medication and a healthful meal plan are two important factors in managing diabetes, physical activity is an equally essential component. Exercise helps your body use insulin efficiently so you can control your blood glucose level more accurately. Staying active also helps you burn calories so you can achieve or maintain a healthful weight. In addition, physical activity reduces the risk of heart disease, high blood pressure, and colon cancer; improves circulation; strengthens bones, muscles, and joints; increases energy; and enhances your sense of well-being. If exercise isn't already a part of your regular routine, here are some suggestions to help get you on the road to a more active lifestyle.

Don't start by heading for the gym. Instead, head to your doctor's office for an "activity prescription." This exercise plan will guide you in deciding what type and amount of physical activity is best for you. Things your doctor should consider in making recommendations include: your current fitness level, the timing of your meal plan, your diabetes medication, and any special health concerns. For example, if you have eye or blood vessel problems, your doctor will advise you on which activities are safe.

One of the keys to sticking with an exercise plan is finding an activity you enjoy. You may want to start with activities such as walking, bicycling, golfing, or swimming. As you become more fit, you can branch out to more strenuous activities, such as rollerblading, step aerobics, or cross-country skiing. Always check with your doctor, however, before changing activities.

Another key to being faithful to your activity routine is to stay flexible in the timing and length of your workouts. Health experts agree that you can benefit from as little as 30 minutes of moderate activity on most—and preferably all—days. But don't feel you have to work out all at one time. Three 10-minute walks are just as good as a 30-minute one. Also, don't forget that everyday activities, such as gardening, mowing the lawn, washing windows, and vigorous housecleaning, count too. If you're just getting into the exercise habit, start slowly, gradually working up to your 30-minute goal.

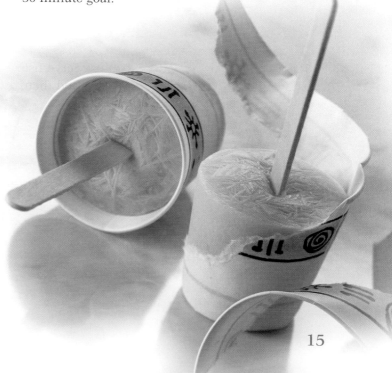

CURE BETWEEN-MEAL
HUNGER PANGS WITH
THESE HEALTHFUL NIBBLES
AND BEVERAGES.

Snacks & Sippers

Pita Chips with
Red Pepper Dip **page 26**

Chèvre and Tomato Spread

THE DELIGHTFUL FLAVORS OF TANGY GOAT CHEESE AND DRIED TOMATOES TEAM UP TO MAKE A SPREAD THAT'S PERFECT FOR ENTERTAINING OR EVERYDAY SNACKING.

⅓ cup dried tomatoes (not oil-packed)

4 ounces soft goat cheese (chèvre)

½ of an 8-ounce package reduced-fat cream cheese (Neufchâtel), softened

¼ cup snipped fresh basil or 2 teaspoons dried basil, crushed

3 cloves garlic, minced

⅛ teaspoon pepper

1 to 2 tablespoons fat-free milk

20 slices party rye bread and/or assorted reduced-fat crackers

Assorted garnishes*

EXCHANGES: ¹/₂ Starch, ¹/₂ High-Fat Meat, ¹/₂ Fat **Prep:** 20 minutes **Chill:** 2 to 4 hours **Makes:** 1¹/₄ cups spread

1 In a small bowl cover dried tomatoes with boiling water. Let stand for 10 minutes. Drain tomatoes, discarding liquid. Finely snip tomatoes.

2 In a medium bowl stir together the snipped tomatoes, goat cheese, cream cheese, basil, garlic, and pepper. Stir in enough of the milk to make the mixture of spreading consistency. Cover and chill in the refrigerator for at least 2 hours or up to 4 hours. Serve on rye bread or crackers. If desired, top with assorted garnishes.

NUTRITION FACTS PER 2 SLICES OF PARTY RYE BREAD AND 2 TABLESPOONS SPREAD: 119 calories, 6 g total fat (3 g saturated fat), 13 mg cholesterol, 248 mg sodium, 11 g carbohydrate, 2 g fiber, 6 g protein.

*Note: Use your choice of fresh vegetables and herbs for garnishes. Quartered cherry tomatoes, small broccoli flowerets, chopped yellow sweet pepper, and fresh basil leaves are shown in the photo.

Roasted Pepper Roll-Ups

THE WHITE KIDNEY BEANS, SPINACH, AND ROASTED RED PEPPERS NESTLED
IN THESE COLORFUL SNACKS ARE AS NUTRITIOUS AS THEY ARE TASTY.

- **1** 15-ounce can white kidney beans (cannellini beans), rinsed and drained
- **½** of an 8-ounce package reduced-fat cream cheese (Neufchâtel), softened
- **¼** cup packed fresh basil
- **1** tablespoon fat-free milk
- **2** small cloves garlic, quartered
- **⅛** teaspoon black pepper
- **⅓** cup roasted red sweet peppers, drained and finely chopped
- **6** 6-inch flour tortillas
- **1** cup packed fresh spinach leaves

EXCHANGES: 1½ Starch, 1 Fat **Prep:** 20 minutes **Chill:** 2 to 24 hours **Makes:** 6 servings

1 For the filling, in a blender container or food processor bowl combine the beans, cream cheese, basil, milk, garlic, and black pepper. Cover and blend or process until smooth. Stir in the roasted peppers.

2 To assemble, spread about ⅓ cup of the filling evenly over each tortilla to within ½ inch of the edge. Arrange spinach leaves over filling to cover. Carefully roll tortillas up tightly. Cover and chill in the refrigerator for at least 2 hours or up to 24 hours.

3 To serve, use a sharp knife to cut roll-ups crosswise into 1½-inch-thick slices.

NUTRITION FACTS PER SERVING: 173 calories, 7 g total fat (3 g saturated fat), 15 mg cholesterol, 289 mg sodium, 24 g carbohydrate, 4 g fiber, 8 g protein.

Curried Cheese Vegetables

TAKE YOUR CHOICE OF COLORFUL CHERRY TOMATOES, BABY PATTYPAN
SQUASH, OR BABY ZUCCHINI TO HOLD THE CREAMY CURRY-AND-CHEESE FILLING.

24 cherry tomatoes, baby
pattypan squash, and/or
baby zucchini halves
½ of an 8-ounce package
reduced-fat cream cheese
(Neufchâtel), softened
½ cup finely shredded carrot

2 tablespoons sliced green
onion
1 tablespoon fat-free milk
½ teaspoon curry powder
⅛ teaspoon garlic powder
Paprika (optional)
Fresh dill (optional)

EXCHANGES: ½ Vegetable, ½ Fat **Start to Finish:** 25 minutes **Makes:** 12 servings

1 Cut a thin layer off the stem end of each cherry tomato. Use a melon baller or a small spoon to hollow out the inside of each tomato or pattypan squash. Invert on paper towels. Use a melon baller or a small spoon to hollow out each zucchini half. Invert on paper towels.

2 In a small bowl stir together cream cheese, carrot, green onion, milk, curry powder, and garlic powder. Spoon mixture into the centers of the hollowed-out vegetables. If desired, sprinkle with paprika and garnish with fresh dill.

NUTRITION FACTS PER SERVING: 33 calories, 2 g total fat (1 g saturated fat), 7 mg cholesterol, 42 mg sodium, 2 g carbohydrate, 1 g fiber, 1 g protein.

Gingered Shrimp Appetizers

ADD A TOUCH OF ELEGANCE TO ANY APPETIZER ASSORTMENT
WITH THESE GINGER-MARINATED SHRIMP WRAPPED IN PEA PODS.

1 pound fresh or frozen large shrimp in shells	**¼** teaspoon finely shredded lemon peel	**¼** teaspoon sugar
1½ cups water	**1** teaspoon lemon juice	Dash salt
4½ teaspoons white wine vinegar	**1** teaspoon grated fresh ginger or ½ teaspoon ground ginger	Dash ground red pepper
1 teaspoon toasted sesame oil or olive oil	**1** clove garlic, minced	**18** to 24 fresh pea pods
		6 to 8 small pieces lemon

EXCHANGES: 1¹/₂ Very Lean Meat **Prep:** 40 minutes **Marinate:** 1 to 2 hours **Makes:** 6 to 8 servings

1 Thaw shrimp, if frozen. Peel and devein shrimp, leaving the tails intact. Rinse shrimp. In a large saucepan bring the water to boiling. Add the shrimp. Cover and simmer for 1 to 3 minutes or until shrimp turn opaque. Drain. Rinse the shrimp with cold water; drain.

2 Place shrimp in a self-sealing plastic bag set in a shallow dish. Add the vinegar, oil, lemon peel, lemon juice, ginger, garlic, sugar, salt, and ground red pepper to bag. Close bag. Marinate in the refrigerator for at least 1 hour or up to 2 hours.

3 Place pea pods in the top of a steamer over boiling water. Cover and steam for 2 to 3 minutes or until the pea pods are just tender. Rinse with cold water; drain.

4 Drain shrimp, discarding marinade. Wrap each shrimp with a pea pod. On six to eight 6-inch skewers, thread lemon pieces and wrapped shrimp.

NUTRITION FACTS PER SERVING: 60 calories, 1 g total fat (0 g saturated fat), 87 mg cholesterol, 123 mg sodium, 2 g carbohydrate, 1 g fiber, 10 g protein.

Pita Chips
with Red Pepper Dip

ROASTED RED SWEET PEPPERS GIVE THIS THYME-ACCENTED DIP A ROBUST FLAVOR THAT
GOES DELICIOUSLY WITH HOMEMADE PITA CHIPS. (PHOTO ON PAGE 17.)

2 medium red sweet peppers
or one 7-ounce jar roasted
red sweet peppers,
drained
2 tablespoons tomato paste
1 teaspoon sugar
1 teaspoon snipped fresh
thyme or $\frac{1}{4}$ teaspoon
dried thyme, crushed

1 clove garlic, minced, or
$\frac{1}{8}$ teaspoon garlic powder
$\frac{1}{4}$ teaspoon salt
Dash ground red pepper
1 recipe Baked Pita Chips

EXCHANGES: $\frac{1}{2}$ Starch, 1 Vegetable **Start to Finish:** 40 minutes **Makes:** 6 servings

1 To roast fresh sweet peppers, cut into quarters lengthwise; remove seeds, membranes, and stems.
Line a baking sheet with foil. Place the peppers, skin sides up, on baking sheet, pressing peppers to
lie flat. Bake in a 425° oven about 20 minutes or until dark and blistered. Remove from oven and
place in a clean paper bag. Close bag and let stand about 10 minutes. When cool enough to handle,
peel peppers; discard skins.

2 Place roasted fresh peppers or drained peppers in a blender container or food processor bowl. Cover;
blend or process until finely chopped. Add tomato paste, sugar, thyme, garlic, salt, and ground red
pepper. Cover; blend until nearly smooth. Serve with Baked Pita Chips. If desired, cover and store
dip in the refrigerator for up to 1 week.

Baked Pita Chips: Split 4 large pita bread rounds in half horizontally. Lightly coat the cut side of each
pita bread half with nonstick cooking spray. Sprinkle each lightly with $\frac{1}{2}$ to $\frac{3}{4}$ teaspoon onion powder, garlic powder, or pepper. Cut each half into 6 wedges. Spread wedges in single layer on a baking
sheet. (You'll need to bake chips in batches.) Bake in a 350° oven for 10 to 12 minutes or until crisp.
If desired, store in an airtight container for up to 1 week.

NUTRITION FACTS PER 2 TABLESPOONS DIP AND 4 CHIPS: 74 calories, 0 g total fat (0 g saturated fat),
0 mg cholesterol, 208 mg sodium, 15 g carbohydrate, 1 g fiber, 3 g protein.

Chocolate-Banana Shake

WHEN YOU SERVE THIS RICH SHAKE, YOUR YOUNGSTERS WILL NEVER COMPLAIN ABOUT DRINKING THEIR MILK. (PICTURED ON PAGE 28.)

1¾ cups fat-free milk
1½ cups vanilla fat-free yogurt
1 small banana, cut into chunks

½ of a 4-serving-size package fat-free instant chocolate pudding mix (about 5 tablespoons)

6 fresh strawberries (optional)
Grated chocolate (optional)

EXCHANGES: ¹/₂ Milk, 1 Fruit **Start to Finish:** 10 minutes **Makes:** 6 (5-ounce) servings

1 In a blender container or food processor bowl combine the milk, yogurt, banana, and pudding mix. Cover and blend or process until smooth. If desired, garnish with strawberries and grated chocolate.

NUTRITION FACTS PER SERVING: 115 calories, 0 g total fat (0 g saturated fat), 2 mg cholesterol, 189 mg sodium, 24 g carbohydrate, 0 g fiber, 5 g protein.

Peach Smoothie **opposite**
Chocolate-Banana Shake **page 27**

Peach Smoothie

USE THIS FROSTY LOW-CAL SHAKE AS A MIDAFTERNOON PICK-ME-UP.

2 fresh medium peeled peaches or unpeeled nectarines, quartered, or ½ of a 16-ounce package frozen unsweetened peach slices

¾ cup fat-free milk
¼ cup frozen orange-pineapple juice concentrate, thawed
2 teaspoons sugar
1 teaspoon vanilla
1 cup ice cubes

EXCHANGES: ½ Milk, ½ Fruit **Start to Finish:** 10 minutes **Makes:** 4 (6-ounce) servings

1 If desired, set aside 4 peach or nectarine slices for garnish. In a blender container combine the remaining peaches or nectarines, the milk, orange-pineapple juice concentrate, sugar, and vanilla. Cover and blend until smooth. Gradually add ice cubes through hole in blender lid, blending until smooth after each addition. If desired, garnish with reserved peach or nectarine slices.

NUTRITION FACTS PER SERVING: 70 calories, 0 g total fat (0 g saturated fat), 1 mg cholesterol, 24 mg sodium, 15 g carbohydrate, 1 g fiber, 2 g protein.

Fruit
Kabobs

WHEN PARTY TIME ROLLS AROUND, THESE FRUITS ON A STICK
ARE A GREAT WAY TO SCOOP UP LOTS OF REFRESHING DIP.

¾ cup cantaloupe chunks

¾ cup honeydew melon
  chunks

¾ cup small strawberries

¾ cup fresh pineapple chunks

2 small bananas, peeled and
  cut into ¾-inch slices

1 cup orange juice

¼ cup lime juice

1 8-ounce carton vanilla
  low-fat or fat-free yogurt

2 tablespoons frozen orange
  juice concentrate, thawed

Ground nutmeg or ground
  cinnamon (optional)

Fresh herb leaves (optional)

EXCHANGES: $1^1/_2$ Fruit **Prep:** 20 minutes **Chill:** 30 minutes to 1 hour **Makes:** 8 servings

1 On eight 6-inch skewers, alternately thread the cantaloupe chunks, honeydew melon chunks, strawberries, pineapple chunks, and banana slices, leaving $^1/_4$-inch space between pieces. Place kabobs in a glass baking dish. In a small bowl combine orange juice and lime juice; pour evenly over kabobs. Cover and chill in the refrigerator for at least 30 minutes or up to 1 hour, turning occasionally.

2 Meanwhile, for dip, in a small bowl stir together the yogurt and orange juice concentrate. Cover and chill in the refrigerator until ready to serve.

3 To serve, arrange the kabobs on a serving platter; discard juice mixture. If desired, sprinkle nutmeg or cinnamon over dip and garnish with herb leaves. Serve dip with kabobs.

NUTRITION FACTS PER 1 KABOB AND 2 TABLESPOONS DIP: 91 calories, 1 g total fat (0 g saturated fat), 2 mg cholesterol, 20 mg sodium, 21 g carbohydrate, 1 g fiber, 2 g protein.

Mango Yogurt Pops

WHEN THE SUMMER HEAT SIZZLES, THESE FRUIT-AND-YOGURT
FROZEN SNACKS WILL PERK UP YOUNG AND OLD ALIKE.

⅓ cup peach nectar or apricot
   nectar
1 teaspoon unflavored gelatin
2 6- or 8-ounce cartons
   vanilla or peach fat-free
   yogurt with sweetener

⅓ of a 26-ounce jar
   refrigerated mango slices,
   drained, or one 8-ounce
   can peach slices, drained

EXCHANGES: ¹/₂ Milk **Prep:** 15 minutes **Freeze:** 4 to 6 hours **Makes:** 8 pops

1 In a small saucepan stir peach or apricot nectar into unflavored gelatin. Let stand for 5 minutes. Cook and stir over medium heat until gelatin is dissolved.

2 In a blender container combine gelatin mixture, yogurt, and drained mango or peach slices. Cover and blend until smooth. Spoon mixture into eight 3-ounce paper cups. Cover each cup with foil. Cut a small slit in the center of each foil cover and insert a rounded wooden stick into each. Freeze pops for at least 4 hours or up to 6 hours or until firm.

3 To serve, remove the foil and tear paper cups away from pops.

NUTRITION FACTS PER POP: 49 calories, 0 g total fat (0 g saturated fat), 1 mg cholesterol, 28 mg sodium, 10 g carbohydrate, 0 g fiber, 2 g protein.

Poultry Pleasers

THESE APPEALING
LOW-FAT AND
LOW-CALORIE MAIN
DISHES, SOUPS, AND
SALADS MAKE THE
MOST OF CHICKEN
AND TURKEY.

Sesame Chicken Kabob Salad **page 96**

Italian Chicken

FOR A TASTE OF THE OLD COUNTRY, SERVE THIS CHICKEN—LOADED WITH BLACK OLIVES, CAPERS, WINE, AND TOMATOES—WITH A TOSSED SALAD AND ITALIAN BREAD.

2 tablespoons olive oil
4 medium skinless, boneless chicken breast halves (about 1 pound total)
1 large onion, halved and thinly slices
2 cloves garlic, minced
3 large tomatoes, coarsely chopped

¼ cup Greek black olives or ripe olives, pitted and sliced
1 tablespoon capers, drained
¼ teaspoon salt
⅛ teaspoon pepper
¼ cup dry red wine or reduced-sodium chicken broth

2 teaspoons cornstarch
¼ cup snipped fresh basil
2 cups hot cooked couscous
Fresh basil sprigs (optional)

EXCHANGES: 1¹/₂ Starch, 2 Vegetable, 3 Lean Meat **Start to Finish:** 40 minutes **Makes:** 4 servings

1 In a large skillet heat 1 tablespoon of the oil over medium-high heat. Add chicken; cook for 4 to 5 minutes on each side or until chicken is tender and no longer pink. Remove from skillet; keep warm.

2 For sauce, add the remaining oil, the onion, and garlic to hot skillet. Cook and stir for 2 minutes. Add the tomatoes, olives, capers, salt, and pepper. Bring to boiling; reduce heat. Cover and simmer for 3 minutes. In a small bowl stir together the wine or broth and cornstarch; add to the skillet. Cook and stir until thickened and bubbly. Cook and stir for 2 minutes more. Stir in snipped basil. Pour sauce over chicken. Serve with couscous. If desired, garnish with basil sprigs.

NUTRITION FACTS PER SERVING: 319 calories, 8 g total fat (2 g saturated fat), 59 mg cholesterol, 289 mg sodium, 32 g carbohydrate, 7 g fiber, 27 g protein.

Roast Tarragon Chicken

ROASTED CHICKEN NEVER TASTED SO GOOD! IF TARRAGON'S ANISELIKE
FLAVOR IS TOO STRONG FOR YOU, SUBSTITUTE ROSEMARY OR THYME INSTEAD.

3 tablespoons olive oil
2½ teaspoons dried tarragon,
   crushed
2 cloves garlic, minced
½ teaspoon coarsely ground
   black pepper
¼ teaspoon salt
1 pound cherry tomatoes
8 small shallots

2½ to 3 pounds meaty chicken
   pieces (breasts, thighs,
   and/or drumsticks)
Fresh tarragon sprigs
   (optional)

EXCHANGES: ½ Vegetable, 1½ Lean Meat, ½ Fat   **Prep:** 15 minutes   **Roast:** 45 minutes   **Makes:** 6 servings

1 In a medium bowl stir together olive oil, dried tarragon, garlic, pepper, and salt. Add tomatoes and shallots; toss gently to coat. Use a slotted spoon to remove tomatoes and shallots from bowl, reserving the olive oil mixture.

2 If desired, skin chicken. Place chicken in a shallow roasting pan. Brush chicken with the reserved olive oil mixture.

3 Roast chicken in a 375° oven for 20 minutes. Add the shallots; roast for 15 minutes. Add the tomatoes; roast for 10 to 12 minutes more or until chicken and vegetables are tender and chicken is no longer pink. If desired, garnish with tarragon sprigs.

NUTRITION FACTS PER SERVING: 227 calories, 13 g total fat (2 g saturated fat), 67 mg cholesterol, 170 mg sodium, 5 g carbohydrate, 1 g fiber, 23 g protein.

Fruit and Chicken Kabobs

THIS SWEET-AND-SASSY MARINADE GIVES THE
COLORFUL KABOBS A BOLD CARIBBEAN FLAVOR.

1 pound skinless, boneless
chicken breast halves
3 tablespoons reduced-
sodium soy sauce
4 teaspoons honey
4 teaspoons red wine vinegar
½ teaspoon curry powder
½ teaspoon ground allspice

¼ teaspoon bottled hot
pepper sauce
1 medium red onion, cut into
1-inch wedges
1 medium nectarine, seeded
and cut into 1-inch pieces,
or 1 medium papaya,
peeled, seeded, and cut
into 1-inch pieces

2 cups hot cooked rice or
couscous
Snipped fresh parsley
(optional)

EXCHANGES: 2 Starch, 1 Fruit, 3 Lean Meat **Prep:** 30 minutes
Marinate: 4 hours **Grill:** 15 minutes **Makes:** 4 servings

1 Cut chicken into 1-inch pieces. Place chicken in a self-sealing plastic bag set in a shallow dish. For marinade, in a small bowl stir together soy sauce, honey, vinegar, curry powder, allspice, and hot pepper sauce. Pour over chicken. Close the bag. Marinate chicken in the refrigerator for 4 hours, turning bag occasionally. Remove chicken from marinade, reserving the marinade.

2 In a saucepan cook the onion in a small amount of boiling water for 3 minutes; drain. On eight 6-inch metal skewers, alternately thread the chicken pieces, nectarine or papaya pieces, and onion wedges, leaving $^1/_4$-inch space between pieces.

3 Place the kabobs on the rack of an uncovered grill. Grill directly over medium-hot coals about 15 minutes or until chicken is tender and no longer pink, turning skewers occasionally. In a small saucepan bring reserved marinade to boiling. Cover and cook for 1 minute. Strain marinade.

4 Brush kabobs with the strained marinade. To serve, divide hot cooked rice or couscous among 4 dinner plates. If desired, sprinkle with parsley. Top rice with kabobs. Pass any remaining marinade.

NUTRITION FACTS PER SERVING: 374 calories, 4 g total fat (1 g saturated fat), 59 mg cholesterol, 462 mg sodium, 54 g carbohydrate, 9 g fiber, 30 g protein.

Chicken with Mushroom Sauce

TO DRESS UP THE SAUCE, USE HALF OF A GREEN AND HALF OF A RED SWEET PEPPER.

Nonstick cooking spray
4 small skinless, boneless
    chicken breast halves
    (about 12 ounces total)
1 teaspoon olive oil
2 cups sliced fresh
    mushrooms
1 medium red or green sweet
    pepper, cut into ¾-inch
    squares

1 clove garlic, minced
½ cup reduced-sodium
    chicken broth
Salt
Black pepper
½ cup fat-free dairy sour cream
1 tablespoon all-purpose flour
⅛ teaspoon black pepper
1 tablespoon dry sherry
    (optional)

2 cups hot cooked white or
    brown rice
Snipped fresh parsley
    (optional)
Fresh chives (optional)
Edible flowers (optional)

EXCHANGES: 2 Starch, 1 Vegetable, 2 Very Lean Meat **Start to Finish:** 25 minutes **Makes:** 4 servings

1 Coat a large nonstick skillet with nonstick cooking spray. Preheat over medium heat. Add chicken and cook about 4 minutes or until browned, turning once. Remove chicken from skillet.

2 Carefully add oil to hot skillet. Cook mushrooms, sweet pepper, and garlic in hot oil until tender. Remove vegetables from skillet; cover with foil to keep warm. Carefully stir chicken broth into skillet. Return chicken to skillet. Sprinkle chicken lightly with salt and black pepper. Bring to boiling; reduce heat. Cover and simmer for 5 to 7 minutes or until chicken is tender and no longer pink. Transfer chicken to a serving platter; cover with foil to keep warm.

3 For sauce, in a small bowl stir together sour cream, flour, and the ⅛ teaspoon black pepper until smooth. If desired, stir in the sherry. Stir sour cream mixture into mixture in skillet. Cook and stir until thickened and bubbly. Cook and stir for 1 minute more. Divide rice among 4 dinner plates; if desired, sprinkle with parsley. Serve chicken, vegetables, and sauce over rice. If desired, garnish with chives and flowers.

NUTRITION FACTS PER SERVING: 259 calories, 4 g total fat (1 g saturated fat), 45 mg cholesterol, 176 mg sodium, 32 g carbohydrate, 1 g fiber, 22 g protein.

Chicken with Pumpkin and Zucchini

ROUND OUT A MEAL FEATURING THIS HEARTY SKILLET STEW WITH A CRISP GREEN SALAD, CRUSTY BREAD, AND FRESH FRUIT FOR DESSERT.

Nonstick cooking spray
2½ to 3 pounds meaty chicken pieces (breasts, thighs, and/or drumsticks), skinned
¼ cup finely chopped onion
2 cloves garlic, minced
2 medium potatoes, peeled and cut in 1-inch cubes

2 cups pumpkin or winter squash peeled and cut into 1-inch cubes
⅔ cup dry white wine or reduced-sodium chicken broth
1 teaspoon dried rosemary, crushed
¼ teaspoon salt

¼ teaspoon pepper
2 medium zucchini, sliced ¼ inch thick
Lemon wedges (optional)
Fresh rosemary sprigs (optional)

EXCHANGES: 1 Starch, ½ Vegetable, 3 Lean Meat **Prep:** 20 minutes **Cook:** 50 minutes **Makes:** 6 servings

1 Coat a 12-inch skillet with nonstick cooking spray. Preheat skillet over medium heat. Cook chicken in hot skillet for 10 to 15 minutes or until lightly brown, turning to brown evenly and adding onion and garlic for the last 5 minutes of cooking. Add the potatoes and pumpkin or winter squash.

2 In a small bowl combine wine or broth, dried rosemary, salt, and pepper; pour over chicken and vegetables. Bring mixture to boiling; reduce heat. Cover and simmer for 25 minutes. Add zucchini. Cover and cook about 5 minutes more or until chicken and vegetables are tender and chicken is no longer pink. Using a slotted spoon, transfer chicken and vegetables to a serving platter. Pass pan juices. If desired, serve with lemon wedges and garnish with rosemary sprigs.

NUTRITION FACTS PER SERVING: 266 calories, 10 g total fat (3 g saturated fat), 66 mg cholesterol, 157 mg sodium, 17 g carbohydrate, 2 g fiber, 22 g protein.

Chicken Burritos

THE COOL-AND-CREAMY SOUR CREAM HELPS KEEP THE HEAT INDEX
OF THESE DYNAMITE CHICKEN BURRITOS FROM CLIMBING TOO HIGH.

½ cup finely chopped plum
   tomato
½ cup finely chopped, peeled
   mango
¼ cup finely chopped red
   onion
4 tablespoons lime juice
3 tablespoons snipped
   fresh cilantro

2 to 3 teaspoons finely
   chopped, seeded jalapeño
   pepper*
12 ounces skinless, boneless
   chicken breast halves
½ cup water
¼ teaspoon salt
⅛ to ¼ teaspoon ground red
   pepper

8 6-inch corn tortillas
1½ cups shredded romaine or
   leaf lettuce
¼ cup light dairy sour cream
   Whole fresh green chile
   peppers (optional)
   Fresh cilantro sprigs
   (optional)

EXCHANGES: 1 Starch, 1 Lean Meat **Start to Finish:** 1 hour **Makes:** 8 burritos

1 For salsa, in a medium bowl combine the tomato, mango, red onion, 2 tablespoons of the lime juice, the snipped cilantro, and the jalapeño pepper. Cover and chill in the refrigerator for 30 minutes.

2 In a large heavy skillet combine the chicken and water. Bring to boiling; reduce heat. Cover and simmer for 12 to 14 minutes or until chicken is tender and no longer pink. Drain well; let cool until easy to handle. Using two forks, shred the chicken. Toss shredded chicken with the remaining lime juice, the salt, and ground red pepper.

3 Meanwhile, wrap the tortillas in foil. Bake in a 350° oven about 10 minutes or until warm.

4 To serve, spoon shredded chicken down the centers of warm tortillas. Top chicken with some of the salsa, the romaine or leaf lettuce, and sour cream. Roll up. Top with remaining salsa. If desired, garnish with green chile peppers and cilantro sprigs.

NUTRITION FACTS PER BURRITO: 129 calories, 2 g total fat (1 g saturated fat), 23 mg cholesterol, 138 mg sodium, 17 g carbohydrate, 1 g fiber, 10 g protein.

*Note: Because chile peppers, such as jalapeños, contain volatile oils that can burn your skin and eyes, avoid direct contact with them as much as possible. When working with chile peppers, wear plastic or rubber gloves. If your bare hands do touch the chile peppers, wash your hands and nails well with soap and water.

Pesto Chicken Breasts with Summer Squash

WITH ONLY FOUR INGREDIENTS, THIS
ASIAGO CHEESE-ACCENTED CHICKEN IS TRUE SIMPLICITY.

2 tablespoons purchased
pesto
4 small skinless, boneless
chicken breast halves
(about 12 ounces total)

2 cups chopped zucchini
and/or yellow summer
squash
2 tablespoons shredded
Asiago or Parmesan cheese

EXCHANGES: 1 Vegetable, 2^1/$_2$ Very Lean Meat, 1^1/$_2$ Fat **Start to Finish:** 15 minutes **Makes:** 4 servings

1 Skim 1 tablespoon oil off pesto (or substitute 1 tablespoon olive oil). In a large nonstick skillet heat oil. Cook chicken in hot oil over medium heat for 4 minutes.

2 Turn the chicken; add zucchini. Cook for 4 to 6 minutes more or until chicken is tender and no longer pink and squash is crisp-tender, stirring squash gently once or twice. Transfer chicken and squash to 4 dinner plates. Spread pesto over chicken; sprinkle with cheese.

NUTRITION FACTS PER SERVING: 169 calories, 8 g total fat (1 g saturated fat), 48 mg cholesterol, 158 mg sodium, 4 g carbohydrate, 1 g fiber, 19 g protein.

Bistro-Style Garlic and Herb Chicken Bundles

**THESE TENDER CHICKEN BREASTS ENCASED IN LAYERS OF FLAKY
PHYLLO DOUGH MAKE THE PERFECT HEADLINER FOR A PARTY MENU.**

Olive oil nonstick cooking
spray
4 medium skinless, boneless
chicken breast halves
(about 1 pound total)
2 cloves garlic, minced

1 tablespoon Dijon-style
mustard or coarse-grain
brown mustard
1½ teaspoons snipped fresh
thyme or ½ teaspoon
dried thyme, crushed

1½ teaspoons snipped fresh
rosemary or ¼ teaspoon
dried rosemary, crushed
6 sheets frozen phyllo dough,
thawed
4 teaspoons plain fine dry
bread crumbs

EXCHANGES: 1 Starch, 3 Lean Meat, ½ Fat **Prep:** 30 minutes **Bake:** 15 minutes **Makes:** 4 servings

1 Coat a large nonstick skillet with nonstick cooking spray. Preheat over medium heat. Add chicken and garlic; cook for 3 to 4 minutes per side or until chicken is evenly browned on both sides. Set aside.

2 In a small bowl combine mustard, thyme, and rosemary. Spread about 1 teaspoon of the mustard mixture over each chicken breast.

3 Coat a baking sheet with nonstick cooking spray. Place 1 phyllo sheet on work surface; coat lightly with nonstick cooking spray. Top with 2 more phyllo sheets, coating each layer with nonstick cooking spray. Cut the stack of phyllo sheets in half lengthwise to form two 17×6½-inch stacks. Place 1 teaspoon bread crumbs along a short edge of each stack. Place 1 chicken breast half crosswise on top of bread crumbs on each stack. Fold long sides over chicken and begin to roll up, starting from the end with the chicken. Transfer bundles to prepared baking sheet. Coat bundles with nonstick cooking spray. Repeat with remaining phyllo and remaining chicken.

4 Bake in a 375° oven for 15 to 20 minutes or until chicken is no longer pink and phyllo is golden brown.

NUTRITION FACTS PER SERVING: 223 calories, 5 g total fat (1 g saturated fat), 59 mg cholesterol, 302 mg sodium, 17 g carbohydrate, 0 g fiber, 24 g protein.

Chicken with Fruit Salsa

COUNT ON THIS SOUTHWESTERN CHICKEN FOR GREAT NUTRITION AND FLAVOR. THE CHIPOTLE PEPPERS ADD LOTS OF SMOKY FLAVOR.

1½ cups finely chopped fresh
    or canned pineapple
1 to 2 canned chipotle
    peppers in adobo sauce,
    drained, seeded, and
    finely chopped
2 tablespoons snipped fresh
    chives

1 tablespoon honey
1 teaspoon finely shredded
    lime peel or lemon peel
2 teaspoons lime juice or
    lemon juice
4 medium skinless, boneless
    chicken breast halves
    (about 1 pound total)

1 teaspoon cooking oil
1 teaspoon dried thyme,
    crushed
¼ teaspoon salt
¼ teaspoon black pepper
    Whole fresh green chile
    peppers (optional)

EXCHANGES: 1 Fruit, 3 Lean Meat **Prep:** 35 minutes **Broil:** 12 minutes **Makes:** 4 servings

1 For salsa, in a medium bowl stir together pineapple, chipotle peppers, chives, honey, lime peel or lemon peel, and lime juice or lemon juice. Let stand at room temperature for 30 minutes.

2 Meanwhile, lightly brush chicken with oil. In a small bowl stir together thyme, salt, and black pepper; rub onto both sides of chicken. Place chicken on the unheated rack of a broiler pan. Broil 4 to 5 inches from heat for 12 to 15 minutes or until chicken is tender and no longer pink, turning once. (Or, lightly grease the unheated rack of an uncovered grill. Place chicken on rack. Grill directly over medium coals for 12 to 15 minutes or until chicken is tender and no longer pink, turning once.) Serve chicken with salsa. If desired, garnish with green chile peppers.

NUTRITION FACTS PER SERVING: 182 calories, 5 g total fat (1 g saturated fat), 59 mg cholesterol, 227 mg sodium, 13 g carbohydrate, 1 g fiber, 22 g protein.

Chicken Teriyaki with Summer Fruit

SUMMER'S JUICY NECTARINES ARE THE PERFECT
PARTNER FOR TERIYAKI-SEASONED GRILLED CHICKEN.

2 cups finely chopped
nectarines, finely chopped
plums, and/or blueberries
2 tablespoons orange
marmalade, melted
1 tablespoon lemon juice or
lime juice
½ teaspoon grated fresh
ginger

¼ teaspoon toasted sesame
oil
Few dashes bottled hot
pepper sauce
1 tablespoon orange
marmalade
1 tablespoon reduced-sodium
teriyaki sauce

4 medium skinless, boneless
chicken breast halves
(about 1 pound total)
Fresh strawberries
(optional)
Flowering kale (optional)
Hot cooked rice (optional)
Snipped fresh parsley
(optional)

EXCHANGES: 1½ Fruit, 3 Very Lean Meat **Prep:** 20 minutes **Grill:** 12 minutes **Makes:** 4 servings

1 In a small bowl stir together the fruit, the 2 tablespoons melted orange marmalade, the lemon juice or lime juice, ginger, sesame oil, and hot pepper sauce. Set aside.

2 In a small bowl stir together the 1 tablespoon orange marmalade and the teriyaki sauce; brush over chicken. Place chicken on the rack of an uncovered grill. Grill directly over medium-hot coals for 12 to 15 minutes or until tender and no longer pink, turning once. (Or, place chicken on the unheated rack of a broiler pan. Broil 4 to 5 inches from heat for 12 to 15 minutes or until tender and no longer pink, turning once.) Serve with the fruit mixture. If desired, garnish with fresh strawberries and kale. If desired, serve with rice sprinkled with parsley.

NUTRITION FACTS PER SERVING: 200 calories, 4 g total fat (1 g saturated fat), 59 mg cholesterol, 136 mg sodium, 20 g carbohydrate, 2 g fiber, 22 g protein.

Garlic-Clove Chicken

DON'T BE ALARMED BY 25 CLOVES OF GARLIC—THEY MELLOW AS THEY BAKE. TO PEEL THE BAKED GARLIC, CUT SKIN AND REMOVE CLOVE WITH THE TIP OF A KNIFE.

Nonstick cooking spray
1½ to 2 pounds meaty chicken
    pieces (breasts, thighs,
    and/or drumsticks),
    skinned
25 cloves garlic (about ½ cup
    or 2 to 3 bulbs)

¼ cup dry white wine
¼ cup reduced-sodium
    chicken broth
Salt
Ground red pepper

EXCHANGES: 1 Vegetable, 3 Lean Meat **Prep:** 20 minutes **Bake:** 45 minutes **Makes:** 4 servings

1 Coat an unheated large skillet with nonstick cooking spray. Preheat over medium heat. Add chicken and cook for 10 minutes, turning to brown evenly. Place chicken in a 2-quart square baking dish. Add unpeeled garlic cloves.

2 In a small bowl combine wine and chicken broth; pour over chicken. Lightly sprinkle chicken with salt and ground red pepper.

3 Cover and bake in a 325° oven for 45 to 50 minutes or until chicken is tender and no longer pink.

NUTRITION FACTS PER SERVING: 184 calories, 6 g total fat (2 g saturated fat), 69 mg cholesterol, 140 mg sodium, 6 g carbohydrate, 0 g fiber, 23 g protein.

Chicken with Chunky Vegetable Sauce

TOMATOES, FRESH OREGANO, ARTICHOKE HEARTS, AND CAPERS TURN ORDINARY CHICKEN INTO A MEDITERRANEAN DELIGHT.

2 tablespoons all-purpose flour
4 medium skinless, boneless chicken breast halves (about 1 pound total)
1 tablespoon olive oil
1 cup finely chopped onion
2 cloves garlic, minced
1 14½-ounce can low-sodium diced tomatoes

1 14-ounce can artichoke hearts, drained and halved
⅓ cup reduced-sodium chicken broth
1 tablespoon snipped fresh oregano or 1 teaspoon dried oregano, crushed
Dash pepper

2 teaspoons drained capers or 2 tablespoons chopped, pitted ripe olives
2 cups hot cooked rice
Kalamata olives or pitted ripe olives (optional)

EXCHANGES: 2 Starch, 1½ Vegetable, 3½ Very Lean Meat, ½ Fat **Start to Finish:** 35 minutes **Makes:** 4 servings

1 Place flour in a shallow dish. Dip chicken in flour to coat. Set aside.

2 In a large skillet heat oil over medium heat. Cook onion in hot oil for 3 minutes. Stir in garlic; push onion mixture to side of skillet. Add chicken. Cook about 4 minutes or until chicken is browned, turning once. Stir in undrained tomatoes, artichoke hearts, broth, dried oregano (if using), and pepper.

3 Bring to boiling; reduce heat. Cover and simmer about 10 minutes or until chicken is tender and no longer pink. Remove chicken; cover and keep warm.

4 Simmer tomato mixture, uncovered, about 3 minutes more or until reduced to desired consistency. Stir in capers or chopped olives and fresh oregano (if using). Serve the chicken over rice. Top with the tomato mixture. If desired, garnish with whole olives.

NUTRITION FACTS PER SERVING: 340 calories, 5 g total fat (1 g saturated fat), 66 mg cholesterol, 502 mg sodium, 39 g carbohydrate, 6 g fiber, 32 g protein.

Skillet Chicken Paella

THIS CHICKEN ADAPTATION OF PAELLA, A SPANISH CLASSIC, IS QUICKER AND EASIER THAN THE TRADITIONAL VERSION.

1 tablespoon olive oil or cooking oil

1¼ pounds skinless, boneless chicken breast halves, cut into bite-size strips

1 medium onion, chopped

2 cloves garlic, minced

2¼ cups reduced-sodium chicken broth

1 cup long grain rice

1 teaspoon dried oregano, crushed

½ teaspoon paprika

¼ teaspoon salt

¼ teaspoon black pepper

⅛ teaspoon ground saffron or ground turmeric

1 14½-ounce can low-sodium stewed tomatoes

1 medium red sweet pepper, cut into bite-size strips

¾ cup frozen peas

EXCHANGES: 2 Starch, 1 Vegetable, 2 Very Lean Meat, $^1/_2$ Fat **Start to Finish:** 40 minutes **Makes:** 6 servings

1 In a 10-inch skillet heat oil. Cook chicken strips, half at a time, in hot oil for 2 to 3 minutes or until no longer pink. Remove from skillet. Set aside.

2 Add onion and garlic to skillet; cook and stir until onion is tender. Add broth, uncooked rice, oregano, paprika, salt, black pepper, and saffron or turmeric. Bring to boiling; reduce heat. Cover and simmer for 15 minutes.

3 Add the undrained stewed tomatoes, sweet pepper, and frozen peas to skillet. Cover and simmer about 5 minutes or until rice is tender. Stir in the cooked chicken. Cook and stir about 1 minute more or until heated through.

NUTRITION FACTS PER SERVING: 285 calories, 6 g total fat (1 g saturated fat), 50 mg cholesterol, 415 mg sodium, 35 g carbohydrate, 2 g fiber, 23 g protein.

Chicken with Peach Salsa

IF YOU CAN'T GET FRESH PEACHES OR PAPAYAS, SUBSTITUTE 1 CUP FROZEN SLICED PEACHES.

2 tablespoons lime juice

4 teaspoons teriyaki sauce or
  soy sauce

4 medium skinless, boneless
  chicken breast halves
  (about 1 pound total)

1 medium peach, peeled,
  pitted, and chopped, or
  ½ of a medium papaya,
  peeled, seeded, and
  chopped (about 1 cup)

1 small chopped tomato
  (½ cup)

2 tablespoons sliced green
  onion

1 tablespoon lime juice

1 teaspoon grated fresh
  ginger or ¼ teaspoon
  ground ginger

¼ teaspoon bottled minced
  garlic or ⅛ teaspoon
  garlic powder

Hot cooked rice (optional)

Fresh thyme sprigs
  (optional)

EXCHANGES: ½ Fruit, 3 Lean Meat **Prep:** 20 minutes

Marinate: 30 minutes to 2 hours **Broil:** 12 minutes **Makes:** 4 servings

1 In a small bowl stir together the 2 tablespoons lime juice and the teriyaki sauce or soy sauce. Brush chicken with the lime juice mixture. Cover and marinate in the refrigerator for at least 30 minutes or up to 2 hours.

2 For salsa, in a medium bowl stir together peach or papaya, tomato, green onion, the 1 tablespoon lime juice, the ginger, and garlic. Cover and chill in the refrigerator for at least 30 minutes or up to 2 hours.

3 Place chicken on the unheated rack of a broiler pan. Broil 4 to 5 inches from the heat for 12 to 15 minutes or until no longer pink, turning once. If desired, serve chicken over hot cooked rice and garnish with thyme. Serve with salsa.

NUTRITION FACTS PER SERVING: 146 calories, 3 g total fat (1 g saturated fat), 59 mg cholesterol, 287 mg sodium, 6 g carbohydrate, 1 g fiber, 22 g protein.

Chicken Cacciatore

FOR A FULLER FLAVOR, USE THE DRY RED WINE INSTEAD OF THE WATER.

Nonstick cooking spray
4 small skinless, boneless chicken breast halves (about 12 ounces total)
1 14½-ounce can stewed tomatoes
1 medium green sweet pepper, cut into thin strips
½ cup sliced fresh mushrooms
¼ cup chopped onion
¼ cup water or dry red wine
2 teaspoons dried Italian seasoning, crushed
⅛ teaspoon black pepper

EXCHANGES: 2 Vegetable, 2 Lean Meat **Prep:** 20 minutes **Cook:** 20 minutes **Makes:** 4 servings

1 Coat a large skillet with nonstick cooking spray. Preheat over medium heat. Add chicken and cook about 6 minutes or until lightly browned, turning to brown evenly.

2 Stir in undrained stewed tomatoes, green sweet pepper, mushrooms, onion, water or wine, Italian seasoning, and black pepper. Bring to boiling; reduce heat. Cover and simmer about 15 minutes or until chicken is tender and no longer pink. Remove chicken from skillet; cover chicken to keep warm. Simmer tomato mixture, uncovered, about 5 minutes more or until desired consistency.

NUTRITION FACTS PER SERVING: 134 calories, 3 g total fat (1 g saturated fat), 45 mg cholesterol, 309 mg sodium, 10 g carbohydrate, 3 g fiber, 18 g protein.

Chicken and Pears with Goat Cheese

BECAUSE SEMISOFT GOAT CHEESES ARE AGED UP TO TWO MONTHS, THEY HAVE A RICH FULL FLAVOR THAT TASTES TERRIFIC WITH CHICKEN AND FRUIT.

8 ounces skinless, boneless chicken breast halves
2 tablespoons water
2 tablespoons balsamic vinegar
1 tablespoon olive oil or salad oil

1 clove garlic, minced
¼ teaspoon salt
¼ teaspoon pepper
8 cups mesclun or torn mixed salad greens
2 medium pears or apples, sliced

2 ounces semisoft goat cheese (chabis), cut into ¼-inch-thick slices
¼ cup coarsely chopped pecans, toasted (optional)

EXCHANGES: ½ Vegetable, 1 Fruit, 2 Lean Meat, 1 Fat **Start to Finish:** 20 minutes **Makes:** 4 servings

1 Place chicken on the unheated rack of a broiler pan. Broil chicken 4 to 5 inches from heat for 12 to 15 minutes or until tender and no longer pink, turning once. (Or, place chicken on the rack of an uncovered grill. Grill directly over medium coals for 12 to 15 minutes or until tender and no longer pink, turning once.) Cut chicken breasts diagonally into thin slices.

2 Meanwhile, for dressing, in a screw-top jar combine the water, vinegar, oil, garlic, salt, and pepper. Cover and shake well. Set aside.

3 Divide mesclun, chicken, pears or apples, and goat cheese among 4 dinner plates. Drizzle with dressing. If desired, sprinkle with pecans.

NUTRITION FACTS PER SERVING: 192 calories, 8 g total fat (1 g saturated fat), 42 mg cholesterol, 218 mg sodium, 17 g carbohydrate, 3 g fiber, 14 g protein.

Tomato-Stuffed Chicken Rolls

PUT TOGETHER A SCRUMPTIOUS YET NUTRITIOUS MEAL BY ADDING PASTA
AND STEAMED ASPARAGUS SPEARS TO THESE HEARTY CHICKEN ROLLS.

4 small skinless, boneless
chicken breast halves
(about 12 ounces total)
1 medium tomato, seeded and
chopped (about ½ cup)
2 tablespoons grated
Parmesan cheese
¼ teaspoon dried Italian
seasoning, oregano, or
basil, crushed

⅛ teaspoon pepper
1 beaten egg white
1 tablespoon water
⅓ cup finely crushed cornflakes
½ teaspoon dried Italian
seasoning, oregano, or
basil, crushed
Nonstick cooking spray

Bottled reduced-sodium
spaghetti sauce, warmed
(optional)
Hot cooked herbed
fettuccine or other pasta
(optional)

EXCHANGES: ½ Vegetable, 2½ Very Lean Meat **Prep:** 20 minutes **Bake:** 20 minutes **Makes:** 4 servings

1 Place each chicken breast half between 2 pieces of plastic wrap. Working from the center to the edges, pound lightly with the flat side of a meat mallet into a rectangle about ⅛ inch thick. Remove plastic wrap.

2 Sprinkle chicken rectangles with the tomato, Parmesan cheese, the ¼ teaspoon herb, and the pepper. Fold in long sides of each chicken rectangle and roll up into a spiral to enclose filling. Secure with wooden toothpicks.

3 In a shallow dish combine the egg white and the water. In another shallow dish combine finely crushed cornflakes and the ½ teaspoon herb. Dip each chicken roll into the egg white mixture. Roll in the cornflake mixture to coat.

4 Coat a 2-quart square baking dish with nonstick cooking spray. Place chicken rolls in dish. Bake in a 400° oven for 20 to 25 minutes or until chicken is tender and no longer pink. Remove toothpicks. If desired, slice chicken rolls and serve with warmed spaghetti sauce over hot cooked pasta.

NUTRITION FACTS PER SERVING: 131 calories, 4 g total fat (1 g saturated fat), 47 mg cholesterol, 162 mg sodium, 5 g carbohydrate, 1 g fiber, 19 g protein.

Oregano Chicken and Vegetables

SPOON THIS EYE-CATCHING SKILLET CHICKEN, SEASONED
WITH OREGANO AND GARLIC, OVER HOT COOKED RICE.

1½ to 2 pounds meaty chicken pieces (breasts, thighs, and/or drumsticks), skinned	½ cup pitted ripe olives, halved	¼ cup dry white wine or chicken broth
¼ teaspoon salt	¼ cup chopped onion	¾ cup chicken broth
⅛ teaspoon black pepper Nonstick cooking spray	¼ cup snipped fresh parsley	1 medium green sweet pepper, cut into strips
1 lemon, thinly sliced	1 tablespoon snipped fresh oregano or 1 teaspoon dried oregano, crushed	1 medium red sweet pepper, cut into strips
1 large tomato, peeled and chopped (¾ cup)	1 clove garlic, minced	Fresh oregano sprigs (optional)
	⅛ teaspoon ground red pepper	

EXCHANGES: 1 Vegetable, 3 Lean Meat, ¹/₂ Fat **Start to Finish:** 45 minutes **Makes:** 4 servings

1 Sprinkle chicken with salt and black pepper. Lightly coat a nonstick skillet with nonstick cooking spray. Preheat over medium heat. Add chicken and cook about 15 minutes or until lightly browned, turning once. Reduce heat.

2 Place half of the lemon slices, half of the tomato, the olives, onion, parsley, snipped or dried oregano, and garlic over chicken pieces in skillet. Sprinkle with ground red pepper. Add the wine or chicken broth and the ³/₄ cup broth. Cover and simmer for 15 minutes.

3 Add the remaining tomato and the sweet peppers. Cover and cook for 5 to 10 minutes more or until sweet peppers are crisp-tender and chicken is tender and no longer pink. Transfer the chicken and vegetables to a platter. Garnish with remaining lemon slices and, if desired, oregano sprigs.

NUTRITION FACTS PER SERVING: 208 calories, 9 g total fat (2 g saturated fat), 69 mg cholesterol, 425 mg sodium, 7 g carbohydrate, 1 g fiber, 24 g protein.

Turkey with Pear-Chipotle Salsa

LEMON AND GARLIC TUCKED UNDER THE SKIN, AS WELL AS AROMATIC WOOD CHIPS, FLAVOR THIS TURKEY BREAST AS IT GRILLS.

4 cups fruit wood or hickory wood chips

1 2- to 2½-pound bone-in turkey breast half with skin

2 teaspoons finely shredded lemon peel

2 cloves garlic, minced

1 to 2 dried chipotle peppers

2 medium pears, cored and finely chopped (about 1½ cups)

2 tablespoons lemon or lime juice

¼ cup snipped dried apricots or dried cranberries

2 tablespoons snipped fresh cilantro

1 tablespoon honey

EXCHANGES: ½ Fruit, 3 Lean Meat **Soak:** 1 hour **Prep:** 20 minutes
Grill: 1½ hours **Stand:** 15 minutes **Makes:** 8 servings

1 At least 1 hour before grilling, soak wood chips in enough water to cover.

2 Loosen turkey skin, leaving it attached at one side, but do not remove. In a small bowl stir together the lemon peel and garlic. Lift turkey skin and rub garlic mixture directly on turkey. Fold skin back over breast to cover as much as possible. Insert a meat thermometer into the thickest part of the turkey breast, making sure the bulb does not touch bone.

3 Drain wood chips. In a covered grill arrange medium-hot coals around a drip pan. Sprinkle about half the chips over the coals. Test for medium heat above pan. Place turkey on grill rack directly over drip pan. Cover and grill for 1½ to 2 hours or until meat thermometer registers 165°, adding remaining chips after about half of the grilling time. Add more coals as necessary to maintain medium heat. Remove turkey from grill and cover with foil. Let stand for 15 minutes before slicing. (The internal temperature will rise about 5° during standing.)

4 Meanwhile, for salsa, wearing plastic gloves, break off and discard pepper stems. In a small bowl just cover peppers with hot water. Let stand 30 minutes. Drain peppers, discarding liquid. Wearing plastic gloves, finely chop peppers.

5 In medium bowl stir together pears and lemon juice or lime juice. Stir in peppers, apricots or cranberries, cilantro, and honey. Let stand, covered, at room temperature for 30 minutes to blend flavors.

6 To serve, remove skin from turkey. Slice turkey; serve with salsa.

NUTRITION FACTS PER SERVING: 186 calories, 6 g total fat (2 g saturated fat), 54 mg cholesterol, 50 mg sodium, 12 g carbohydrate, 2 g fiber, 21 g protein.

Apricot-Stuffed Grilled Turkey Breast

KITCHEN SHEARS MAKE QUICK WORK OF SNIPPING DRIED APRICOTS.

1 2- to 2½-pound bone-in turkey breast half
1½ cups soft bread crumbs (2 slices)
½ cup snipped dried apricots
¼ cup chopped pecans, toasted

2 tablespoons apple juice or water
1 tablespoon cooking oil
¼ teaspoon garlic salt
¼ teaspoon dried rosemary, crushed

1 tablespoon Dijon-style mustard
1 tablespoon water

EXCHANGES: ¹/₂ Starch, ¹/₂ Fruit, 3 Lean Meat **Prep:** 25 minutes
Grill: 1 hour **Stand:** 15 minutes **Makes:** 8 servings

1 In a small bowl cover 4 or 5 wooden toothpicks with water. Set aside. Remove bone from turkey breast. Cut a horizontal slit into thickest part of turkey breast to form a 5×4-inch pocket. Set aside.

2 In a medium bowl combine bread crumbs, apricots, pecans, apple juice or water, oil, garlic salt, and rosemary. Spoon stuffing mixture into pocket in turkey breast. Securely fasten the opening with water-soaked wooden toothpicks. Stir together mustard and water. Set aside.

3 In a covered grill arrange medium-hot coals around a drip pan. Test for medium heat above pan. Place turkey on the grill rack directly over drip pan. Cover and grill about 1 hour or until turkey juices run clear (an instant-read thermometer inserted into stuffing should register 165°), brushing often with mustard mixture during the last 15 minutes of grilling. Remove turkey from grill and cover with foil. Let stand for 15 minutes before slicing. (The internal temperature will rise about 5° during standing.) Discard any remaining mustard mixture.

NUTRITION FACTS PER SERVING: 237 calories, 11 g total fat (2 g saturated fat), 59 mg cholesterol, 205 mg sodium, 10 g carbohydrate, 1 g fiber, 24 g protein.

Turkey with Tomato Relish

SALSA-FLAVORED CRACKERS MAKE A CRISPY CRUMB COATING FOR SUCCULENT TURKEY STEAKS.

Nonstick cooking spray
½ cup finely crushed reduced-fat salsa-flavored or reduced-fat cheese-flavored crackers
¼ teaspoon ground cumin
¼ teaspoon celery seeds
4 turkey breast tenderloin steaks (about 12 ounces total)*

1 tablespoon butter or margarine, melted
1 14½-ounce can diced tomatoes, drained
1 4½-ounce can diced green chili peppers, drained
½ cup finely chopped onion
2 to 4 tablespoons snipped fresh cilantro
1 tablespoon vinegar

1 teaspoon sugar
⅛ teaspoon salt
Fresh cilantro sprigs (optional)

EXCHANGES: 2 Vegetable, 2 Lean Meat **Prep:** 20 minutes **Bake:** 30 minutes **Makes:** 4 servings

1 Coat a 2-quart rectangular baking dish with nonstick cooking spray. Set aside. In a shallow dish combine crushed crackers, cumin, and celery seeds. Coat turkey with cracker mixture. Place in the prepared dish. Drizzle with the melted butter or margarine. Bake, uncovered, in a 375° oven about 30 minutes or until turkey is tender and no longer pink.

2 Meanwhile, for relish, in a medium bowl combine the drained tomatoes, chili peppers, onion, and snipped cilantro. Stir in the vinegar, sugar, and salt. Cover and chill in the refrigerator until serving time. Serve turkey with the relish. If desired, garnish with cilantro sprigs.

NUTRITION FACTS PER SERVING: 164 calories, 6 g total fat (2 g saturated fat), 45 mg cholesterol, 490 mg sodium, 11 g carbohydrate, 1 g fiber, 18 g protein.

*Note: If you can't find turkey breast tenderloin steaks, buy two turkey breast tenderloins and split them in half lengthwise.

Vegetable-Stuffed Turkey Roll

A PARMESAN CHEESE-AND-VEGETABLE FILLING GIVES TURKEY LOAF A NEW TWIST.

1 beaten egg	**¼** teaspoon black pepper	**2** tablespoons currant jelly,
½ cup fine dry bread crumbs	**1½** pounds uncooked ground	melted
½ cup finely chopped onion	turkey	Carrot curls (optional)
¼ cup fat-free milk	**1** cup chopped fresh broccoli	Fresh parsley sprigs
½ teaspoon dried thyme,	**⅔** cup shredded carrot	(optional)
crushed	**⅓** cup chopped red sweet	
¼ teaspoon dried rosemary,	pepper	
crushed	**2** tablespoons grated	
¼ teaspoon garlic salt	Parmesan cheese	

EXCHANGES: 1 Starch, ¹/₂ Vegetable, 3 Lean Meat **Prep:** 25 minutes **Bake:** 1 hour **Makes:** 6 servings

1 In a medium bowl combine egg, bread crumbs, onion, milk, thyme, rosemary, garlic salt, and black pepper. Add turkey; mix well. On waxed paper pat turkey mixture into a 12×8-inch rectangle. Set aside.

2 In a covered small saucepan cook broccoli, carrot, and red pepper in a small amount of boiling water for 3 to 4 minutes or until crisp-tender.* Drain well. Stir in Parmesan cheese.

3 Spread vegetable mixture over turkey mixture to within 1 inch of edges. Beginning at a short end, roll turkey tightly into a spiral, using waxed paper to lift mixture. Peel waxed paper away as you roll. Place in a 9×5×3-inch loaf pan. Bake in a 350° oven for 1 to 1¹/₄ hours or until done (165°).** Remove from pan; transfer to a serving platter. Brush with melted jelly. If desired, garnish with carrot curls and parsley.

NUTRITION FACTS PER SERVING: 266 calories, 11 g total fat (3 g saturated fat), 127 mg cholesterol, 255 mg sodium, 16 g carbohydrate, 2 g fiber, 24 g protein.

*Note: To cook stuffing in a microwave oven, in a 1-quart microwave-safe casserole combine the broccoli, carrot, and red pepper. Microwave on 100% power (high) for 2 to 3 minutes or until crisp-tender; drain. Stir in Parmesan cheese.

**Note: The internal color of a ground turkey loaf is not a reliable doneness indicator. A turkey or chicken loaf cooked to 165°, regardless of color, is safe. Use an instant-read thermometer to check the internal temperature. To measure the doneness of the loaf, insert an instant-read thermometer into the center of the loaf to a depth of 2 to 3 inches.

Chicken Tortellini Soup

CHICKEN NOODLE SOUP TAKES ON AN ITALIAN ACCENT WHEN THE NOODLES ARE REPLACED BY PLUMP CHEESE TORTELLINI.

12 ounces skinless, boneless chicken breast halves
2 teaspoons olive oil
3 cloves garlic, minced
2 14-ounce cans reduced-sodium chicken broth
3 cups sliced fresh mushrooms
1¾ cups water

2 medium carrots, cut into bite-size strips (1 cup)
2 cups packed torn fresh purple kale or spinach
1 teaspoon dried tarragon, crushed
1 9-ounce package refrigerated cheese-filled tortellini

EXCHANGES: 1 Starch, 2 Vegetable, 2 Lean Meat **Start to Finish:** 40 minutes **Makes:** 6 servings

1 Cut the chicken into ³/₄-inch pieces. In a Dutch oven heat oil over medium-high heat. Cook and stir chicken and garlic in hot oil for 5 to 6 minutes or until chicken is no longer pink. Stir in chicken broth, mushrooms, the water, carrots, kale (if using), and tarragon.

2 Bring mixture to boiling; reduce heat. Cover and simmer for 2 minutes. Add tortellini. Cover and simmer for 5 to 6 minutes more or until tortellini is tender. Stir in the spinach (if using).

NUTRITION FACTS PER SERVING: 254 calories, 7 g total fat (2 g saturated fat), 50 mg cholesterol, 596 mg sodium, 27 g carbohydrate, 3 g fiber, 21 g protein.

Five-Spice Chicken Noodle Soup

SOY SAUCE, FIVE-SPICE POWDER, AND GINGER GIVE THIS ASIAN-INSPIRED
SOUP LOTS OF FLAVOR WITHOUT LOTS OF CALORIES AND FAT.

2½ cups water	**2** cloves garlic, minced	**2** ounces dried somen
1¼ cups reduced-sodium	**¼** teaspoon five-spice powder	noodles, broken into
chicken broth	**⅛** teaspoon ground ginger	2-inch lengths, or
2 green onions, thinly	**2** cups chopped bok choy	2 ounces dried fine
bias-sliced	**1** medium red sweet pepper,	noodles
2 teaspoons reduced-sodium	thinly sliced into strips	**1½** cups chopped cooked
soy sauce		chicken (about 8 ounces)

EXCHANGES: ½ Starch, 1 Vegetable, 2 Lean Meat **Start to Finish:** 20 minutes **Makes:** 4 servings

1 In a large saucepan combine water, chicken broth, green onions, soy sauce, garlic, five-spice powder, and ginger. Bring to boiling. Stir in bok choy, sweet pepper strips, and noodles. Return to boiling; reduce heat. Boil gently, uncovered, for 3 to 5 minutes or until noodles are just tender. Stir in the cooked chicken. Heat through.

NUTRITION FACTS PER SERVING: 181 calories, 4 g total fat (1 g saturated fat), 51 mg cholesterol, 556 mg sodium, 14 g carbohydrate, 1 g fiber, 20 g protein.

Kale, Lentil, and Chicken Soup

LEAFY GREEN KALE, RED LENTILS, AND TOMATO ADD NUTRIENTS
AS WELL AS GREAT TASTE TO THIS HEARTY HOME-STYLE SOUP.

1 tablespoon olive oil
1 cup chopped onion
1 cup coarsely chopped carrots
2 cloves garlic, minced
6 cups reduced-sodium chicken broth*

1 tablespoon snipped fresh basil or 1 teaspoon dried basil, crushed (optional)
4 cups coarsely chopped kale (about 8 ounces)
⅛ teaspoon pepper

1½ cups cubed cooked chicken (about 8 ounces)
1 medium tomato, seeded and chopped
½ cup dry red lentils

EXCHANGES: ½ Starch, 2½ Vegetable, 2 Very Lean Meat, ½ Fat **Start to Finish:** 45 minutes **Makes:** 6 servings

1 In a large saucepan heat oil over medium-low heat. Add onion, carrots, and garlic. Cover and cook for 5 to 7 minutes or until vegetables are nearly tender, stirring occasionally.

2 Add broth and dried basil (if using) to vegetable mixture. Bring to boiling; reduce heat. Cover and simmer for 10 minutes. Stir in kale, salt, and pepper. Return to boiling; reduce heat. Cover and simmer for 10 minutes.

3 Stir in chicken, tomato, lentils, and fresh basil (if using). Cover and simmer for 5 to 10 minutes more or until kale and lentils are tender.

NUTRITION FACTS PER SERVING: 195 calories, 5 g total fat (1 g saturated fat), 31 mg cholesterol, 680 mg sodium, 19 g carbohydrate, 4 g fiber, 19 g protein.

*Note: If sodium is of concern, lower the sodium in this recipe by substituting low-sodium chicken broth for the reduced-sodium chicken broth. Or, prepare your own lightly salted chicken broth. You may need to experiment with additional seasonings to achieve a soup with well-rounded flavor.

Chicken and Prosciutto Roll-Ups

THIS ADAPTATION OF THE ITALIAN CLASSIC—BRACIOLA—WRAPS CHICKEN, INSTEAD OF MEAT, AROUND ITALIAN HAM, FONTINA CHEESE, AND ROASTED PEPPERS.

¼ cup white wine
2 teaspoons snipped fresh thyme or ½ teaspoon dried thyme, crushed
4 medium skinless, boneless chicken breast halves (about 1 pound total)

4 thin slices prosciutto (Italian ham), trimmed of fat
2 ounces fontina cheese, thinly sliced
½ of a 7-ounce jar roasted red sweet peppers, cut into thin strips (about ½ cup)

Hot cooked spinach fettuccine (optional)
Fresh thyme sprigs (optional)

EXCHANGES: ½ Vegetable, 3½ Lean Meat **Prep:** 25 minutes **Grill:** 15 minutes **Makes:** 4 servings

1 For sauce, in a small bowl combine wine and the snipped or dried thyme. Set aside.

2 Place a chicken breast half between 2 pieces of plastic wrap. Using the flat side of a meat mallet, pound the chicken lightly into a rectangle about ⅛ inch thick. Remove plastic wrap. Repeat with remaining chicken breast halves.

3 Place a slice of prosciutto and one-fourth of the cheese on each chicken piece. Arrange one-fourth of the roasted peppers on cheese near bottom edge of chicken. Starting from bottom edge, roll up into a spiral; secure with wooden toothpicks. (If desired, wrap chicken rolls in plastic wrap and chill in the refrigerator for up to 4 hours.)

4 Lightly grease the unheated rack of an uncovered grill. Place chicken on the rack. Grill directly over medium coals for 15 to 17 minutes or until chicken is tender and no longer pink, turning to cook evenly. Brush twice with sauce during the last 5 minutes of grilling. If desired, serve with fettuccine. If desired, garnish with thyme sprigs. To serve, slice each chicken breast.

NUTRITION FACTS PER SERVING: 214 calories, 9 g total fat (4 g saturated fat), 76 mg cholesterol, 294 mg sodium, 2 g carbohydrate, 0 g fiber, 27 g protein.

Chicken, Pear, and Blue Cheese Salad

A QUICK STOP AT THE DELI COUNTER FOR ROASTED CHICKEN TAKES MOST OF THE WORK OUT OF THIS SOPHISTICATED SALAD.

6 cups torn mixed salad greens or mesclun (about 8 ounces)

10 to 12 ounces roasted or grilled chicken breast, cut into bite-size pieces

¾ cup bottled reduced-calorie or regular blue cheese salad dressing

2 ripe pears, cored and sliced Freshly ground black pepper (optional)

EXCHANGES: 1 Vegetable, 1 Fruit, 3 Very Lean Meat, ¹/₂ Fat **Start to Finish:** 15 minutes **Makes:** 4 servings

1 In a large bowl combine the salad greens or mesclun, chicken, and salad dressing; toss gently to coat. Divide among 4 individual salad bowls or dinner plates. Arrange pear slices on top of salads. If desired, sprinkle with pepper.

NUTRITION FACTS PER SERVING: 208 calories, 6 g total fat (2 g saturated fat), 72 mg cholesterol, 591 mg sodium, 18 g carbohydrate, 3 g fiber, 23 g protein.

Fruit and Chicken Salad

BECAUSE FROZEN JUICE CONCENTRATES PROVIDE A GREAT DEAL OF FLAVOR
AND BODY, THEY ARE IDEAL FOR MAKING LOW-FAT SALAD DRESSINGS.

½ cup fat-free dairy
   sour cream
½ cup fat-free mayonnaise
   dressing or salad dressing
1 tablespoon frozen orange
   juice concentrate, thawed
⅛ teaspoon ground ginger
   Dash ground red pepper

3 green onions, sliced
2 cups thinly sliced celery
1½ cups seedless red or green
   grapes, halved
1½ cups chopped cooked
   chicken (about 8 ounces)
½ cup dried apricots, cut into
   slivers

Lettuce leaves (optional)
2 plum tomatoes, thinly sliced
1 cucumber, thinly sliced

EXCHANGES: 2 Vegetable, 2 Fruit, 2 Lean Meat **Prep:** 25 minutes **Chill:** 2 to 4 hours **Makes:** 4 servings

1 For dressing, stir together the sour cream, mayonnaise dressing or salad dressing, orange juice concentrate, ginger, and ground red pepper. Stir in green onions.

2 In a large bowl toss together celery, grapes, chicken, and apricots; stir in the dressing. Cover and chill in the refrigerator for at least 2 hours or up to 4 hours.

3 To serve, if desired, line 4 salad plates with lettuce leaves. Arrange tomatoes and cucumber on plates. Top with chicken mixture.

NUTRITION FACTS PER SERVING: 264 calories, 3 g total fat (1 g saturated fat), 44 mg cholesterol, 511 mg sodium, 40 g carbohydrate, 5 g fiber, 21 g protein.

Grilled Chicken and Rice Salad

DRIZZLE THIS VERSATILE THYME VINAIGRETTE OVER YOUR FAVORITE CHEF'S SALAD TOO.

12 ounces skinless, boneless chicken breast halves or thighs
1 recipe Thyme Vinaigrette
1 cup loose-pack frozen French-cut green beans
2 cups cooked brown rice and wild rice blend, chilled

1 14-ounce can artichoke hearts, drained and quartered
1 cup shredded red cabbage
½ cup shredded carrot
1 green onion, sliced
Lettuce leaves (optional)

EXCHANGES: 1½ Starch, 2 Vegetable, 2½ Very Lean Meat, 1½ Fat
Start to Finish: 30 minutes **Makes:** 4 servings

1 Brush chicken with 2 tablespoons of the Thyme Vinaigrette. Set aside the remaining vinaigrette.

2 Place chicken on the rack of an uncovered grill. Grill directly over medium coals for 12 to 15 minutes or until chicken is tender and no longer pink, turning once. (Or, place chicken on unheated rack of a broiler pan. Broil 4 to 5 inches from the heat for 12 to 15 minutes or until chicken is tender and no longer pink, turning once.) Cut chicken into bite-size strips.

3 Meanwhile, rinse green beans with cool water for 30 seconds; drain well. In large bowl toss together beans, cooked rice, artichoke hearts, cabbage, carrot, and green onion. Pour the remaining vinaigrette over rice mixture; gently toss to coat.

4 If desired, arrange lettuce leaves on 4 dinner plates. Top with the rice mixture and chicken.

Thyme Vinaigrette: In a screw-top jar combine ¼ cup white wine vinegar; 2 tablespoons olive oil; 2 tablespoons water; 1 tablespoon grated Parmesan cheese; 2 teaspoons snipped fresh thyme; 1 clove garlic, minced; and ¼ teaspoon pepper. Cover and shake well.

NUTRITION FACTS PER SERVING: 322 calories, 9 g total fat (2 g saturated fat), 50 mg cholesterol, 397 mg sodium, 33 g carbohydrate, 7 g fiber, 25 g protein.

Szechwan Chicken Salad

THIS ASIAN SALAD FEATURES JICAMA, CARROT, CUCUMBERS, ENOKI MUSHROOMS, AND A SPRINKLING OF PEANUTS.

2 teaspoons cooking oil
1 teaspoon toasted sesame oil
2 tablespoons grated fresh ginger
3 cloves garlic, minced
⅓ cup rice vinegar or white wine vinegar
3 tablespoons water
2 tablespoons reduced-sodium soy sauce

4 small skinless, boneless chicken breast halves (about 12 ounces total)
2 tablespoons water
1 fresh jalapeño pepper, seeded and chopped*
½ teaspoon sugar
1 medium carrot, cut into bite-size strips
1 cup peeled jicama cut into bite-size strips

Lettuce leaves (optional)
2 medium cucumbers, quartered lengthwise and cut into ¼-inch slices
1⅓ cups enoki mushrooms
2 green onions, sliced
2 tablespoons chopped unsalted cocktail peanuts

EXCHANGES: 3 Vegetable, 2 Lean Meat **Prep:** 25 minutes
Marinate: 4 to 24 hours **Grill:** 12 minutes **Makes:** 4 servings

1 In a small saucepan heat cooking oil and sesame oil over medium-high heat for 1 minute. Cook and stir ginger and garlic in hot oil for 15 seconds. Remove saucepan from heat; stir in the vinegar, the 3 tablespoons water, and the soy sauce. Cool completely.

2 Place chicken in a self-sealing plastic bag set in a shallow dish. Pour half of the soy mixture over the chicken; reserve remaining soy mixture. Close bag. Marinate in the refrigerator for at least 4 hours or up to 24 hours.

3 Meanwhile, for dressing, in a small bowl stir together reserved soy mixture, the 2 tablespoons water, the jalapeño pepper, and sugar. Cover and chill in the refrigerator for at least 4 hours or up to 24 hours.

4 Drain chicken, discarding marinade. Lightly grease the unheated rack of an uncovered grill. Place chicken on rack. Grill directly over medium coals for 12 to 15 minutes or until chicken is tender and no longer pink, turning once. Slice chicken into bite-size pieces. Combine the carrot and jicama.

5 To serve, if desired, line 4 salad plates with lettuce leaves. Top with carrot mixture, cucumbers, chicken, mushrooms, green onions, and peanuts. Stir dressing; drizzle 1 tablespoon of the dressing over each serving.

NUTRITION FACTS PER SERVING: 200 calories, 7 g total fat (1 g saturated fat), 45 mg cholesterol, 231 mg sodium, 15 g carbohydrate, 3 g fiber, 20 g protein.

*Note: Because chile peppers, such as jalapeños, contain volatile oils that can burn your skin and eyes, avoid direct contact with them as much as possible. When working with chile peppers, wear plastic or rubber gloves. If your bare hands do touch the chile peppers, wash your hands and nails well with soap and warm water.

Sesame Chicken Kabob Salad

THIS FESTIVE SALAD BRINGS YOU SWEET-AND-SOUR
CHICKEN IN A NEW FORM. (PHOTO ON PAGE 35.)

8 6- to 8-inch wooden
   skewers
4 medium skinless, boneless
   chicken breast halves
   (about 1 pound total)
16 fresh pineapple chunks
   (about 1 cup)
1 medium yellow sweet
   pepper, cut into 1-inch
   pieces

3 tablespoons rice vinegar or
   white wine vinegar
2 tablespoons water
1 tablespoon salad oil
1 tablespoon soy sauce
1 teaspoon toasted
   sesame oil
½ teaspoon dry mustard
1 tablespoon bottled
   plum sauce or bottled
   chili sauce

2 cups chopped red cabbage
2 cups chopped bok choy or
   iceberg lettuce
16 to 24 snow peas, strings
   and tips removed
½ cup sliced fresh
   mushrooms
¼ cup sliced red radishes

EXCHANGES: 1½ Vegetable, ½ Fruit, 4 Very Lean Meat, 1 Fat
Prep: 40 minutes **Grill:** 10 minutes **Makes:** 4 servings

1 Soak wooden skewers in enough water to cover for 30 minutes; drain. Meanwhile, cut each chicken breast half into 4 lengthwise strips. On soaked skewers, alternately thread chicken, pineapple chunks, and pepper pieces, leaving ¼-inch space between pieces.

2 For dressing, in a screw-top jar combine vinegar, water, salad oil, soy sauce, sesame oil, and dry mustard. Cover and shake well. Reserve 2 tablespoons of the dressing. Cover remaining dressing; chill in the refrigerator until needed.

3 Stir together the reserved dressing and the plum sauce or chili sauce. Brush over kabobs.

4 Place kabobs on the rack of an uncovered grill. Grill directly over medium coals for 10 to 12 minutes or until chicken is tender and no longer pink, turning once.

5 In a large bowl combine cabbage, bok choy or lettuce, snow peas, mushrooms, and radishes. Divide greens mixture among 4 dinner plates. Top with kabobs. Shake dressing; drizzle over salads.

NUTRITION FACTS PER SERVING: 246 calories, 7 g total fat (1 g saturated fat), 66 mg cholesterol, 328 mg sodium, 15 g carbohydrate, 3 g fiber, 30 g protein.

Curried Chicken and Grapefruit Salad

NEXT TIME, USE GARAM MASALA, AN EAST INDIAN SEASONING, INSTEAD OF CURRY POWDER.

½ teaspoon curry powder
1 clove garlic, minced
4 medium skinless, boneless
 chicken breast halves
 (about 1 pound total)
 Nonstick cooking spray
1 large grapefruit
 Grapefruit juice

1 tablespoon salad oil
1 tablespoon Dijon-style
 mustard
1 tablespoon honey
⅛ teaspoon pepper
6 cups torn fresh spinach
2 large green onions, sliced
 (¼ cup)

EXCHANGES: 1 Vegetable, ½ Fruit, 4 Very Lean Meat, ½ Fat **Start to Finish:** 25 minutes **Makes:** 4 servings

1 Combine curry powder and garlic; sprinkle onto both sides of chicken, pressing into surface. Lightly coat a nonstick skillet with nonstick cooking spray. Preheat skillet over medium-high heat. Add chicken; cook for 8 to 10 minutes or until chicken is no longer pink, turning once. Transfer chicken to a clean cutting board; keep warm.

2 For dressing, peel grapefruit. Section and seed grapefruit over a medium bowl, catching any juices in the bowl. Add enough additional grapefruit juice to measure 3 tablespoons. In a screw-top jar combine grapefruit juice, oil, mustard, honey, and pepper. Cover and shake well.

3 Slice chicken across the grain into ½-inch-wide strips. Divide spinach among 4 dinner plates. Arrange chicken and grapefruit sections on top of spinach. Drizzle each serving with dressing and sprinkle with green onions.

NUTRITION FACTS PER SERVING: 213 calories, 6 g total fat (1 g saturated fat), 66 mg cholesterol, 157 mg sodium, 12 g carbohydrate, 5 g fiber, 29 g protein.

Strawberry-Peppercorn Vinaigrette with Turkey

WAKE-UP YOUR TASTE BUDS WITH THIS ROSY SALAD DRESSING THAT COMBINES SWEET STRAWBERRIES WITH FIERY BLACK PEPPER.

8 cups mesclun or 6 cups torn romaine and 2 cups torn curly endive, chicory, and/or escarole

2½ cups cooked turkey or chicken, cut into bite-size strips (about 12 ounces)

2 cups sliced, peeled kiwi fruit and/or sliced carambola (star fruit)

1½ cups enoki mushrooms (3 ounces)

1 cup red cherry tomatoes and/or yellow baby pear tomatoes, halved

1 recipe Strawberry-Peppercorn Vinaigrette

EXCHANGES: 1½ Vegetable, ½ Fruit, 3½ Lean Meat   **Start to Finish:** 25 minutes   **Makes:** 4 servings

1 Place mesclun or romaine and endive in a large serving bowl or colander. Top with turkey, kiwi fruit, mushrooms, and tomatoes. Serve with Strawberry-Peppercorn Vinaigrette.

Strawberry-Peppercorn Vinaigrette: In a food processor bowl or blender container combine 1 cup cut-up fresh or frozen strawberries (thaw frozen strawberries), 2 tablespoons red wine vinegar, and ⅛ teaspoon cracked black pepper. Cover and process or blend until smooth.

NUTRITION FACTS PER SERVING: 251 calories, 8 g total fat (2 g saturated fat), 84 mg cholesterol, 102 mg sodium, 15 g carbohydrate, 5 g fiber, 31 g protein.

Warm Chinese Chicken Salad

PART OF THE CHARM OF THIS MAIN DISH SALAD IS THE
RICH, NUTTY FLAVOR OF THE TOASTED SESAME OIL.

½ cup reduced-sodium
  chicken broth
1 teaspoon minced garlic
½ teaspoon crushed
  red pepper
12 ounces skinless, boneless
  chicken breast halves
3 tablespoons rice vinegar
2 tablespoons reduced-
  sodium soy sauce

1 tablespoon honey
1 tablespoon toasted
  sesame oil
1 teaspoon minced fresh
  ginger
4 cups packed shredded
  Chinese cabbage or napa
1 medium red or yellow sweet
  pepper, cut into thin strips

2 green onions, bias-sliced
  into ½-inch pieces
1 to 2 tablespoons sliced
  almonds, toasted
Orange half-slices (optional)
Fresh chives (optional)

EXCHANGES: ½ Vegetable, 2½ Lean Meat, 1 Fat **Start to Finish:** 25 minutes **Makes:** 4 servings

1 In a 10-inch skillet combine broth, garlic, and crushed red pepper. Bring to boiling; reduce heat. Add chicken. Cover and simmer about 10 minutes or until chicken is tender and no longer pink; drain.

2 Meanwhile, in a small bowl combine vinegar, soy sauce, honey, sesame oil, and ginger; mix well. Combine cabbage and sweet pepper; toss with ¼ cup of the vinegar mixture. Arrange on 4 plates.

3 Shred, slice, or chop warm chicken; toss with remaining vinegar mixture. Arrange over cabbage mixture; top with green onions and almonds. If desired, garnish with orange slices and chives.

NUTRITION FACTS PER SERVING: 178 calories, 7 g total fat (1 g saturated fat), 45 mg cholesterol, 395 mg sodium, 11 g carbohydrate, 1 g fiber, 19 g protein.

Meat
Entrées

BUILD SENSATIONAL
MEALS YOUR WHOLE
FAMILY WILL ENJOY
AROUND THESE
TEMPTING BEEF,
VEAL, AND PORK
FAVORITES.

Garlic Steaks with Nectarine-Onion Relish **page 110**

Citrus-Tequila
Fajitas

**THE CITRUS AND TEQUILA MARINADE TENDERIZES THE
FLANK STEAK WHILE GIVING IT SOME SOUTH-OF-THE-BORDER ZING.**

12 ounces beef flank steak	**½** teaspoon dried oregano, crushed	**½** of a medium red or yellow sweet pepper, cut into strips
3 tablespoons frozen orange juice concentrate, thawed	**1** clove garlic, minced	**½** of a small onion, sliced and separated into rings
3 tablespoons tequila or water	**⅛** teaspoon salt	Sliced fresh chile peppers (optional)
2 tablespoons lime juice	**⅛** teaspoon ground red pepper	
1 teaspoon grated fresh ginger	**8** small corn or four 8- to 10-inch flour tortillas	

EXCHANGES: 1 Starch, 1 Vegetable, ½ Fruit, 2 Lean Meat **Prep:** 10 minutes
Marinate: 4 hours **Broil:** 15 minutes **Makes:** 4 servings

1 Score both sides of beef in a diamond pattern by making shallow diagonal cuts at 1-inch intervals. Place beef in a self-sealing plastic bag set in a shallow dish.

2 For marinade, in a small bowl stir together orange juice concentrate, tequila or water, lime juice, ginger, oregano, garlic, salt, and ground red pepper. Pour over meat in bag. Close bag. Marinate in the refrigerator for 4 hours, turning bag occasionally.

3 Drain beef, reserving marinade. Place meat on the unheated rack of a broiler pan. Broil meat 4 to 5 inches from the heat for 15 to 18 minutes or until medium doneness (160°), turning once. [Or, place meat on the rack of an uncovered grill. Grill directly over medium coals for 17 to 21 minutes or until medium doneness (160°), turning once.] Thinly slice meat diagonally across the grain.

4 To warm tortillas, wrap in foil. Place beside broiler pan or on grill rack for the last 8 minutes of cooking meat.

5 Meanwhile, in a small saucepan combine reserved marinade, sweet pepper strips, and onion. Bring to boiling; reduce heat. Simmer, uncovered, for 3 to 5 minutes or until vegetables are tender.

6 To serve, fill warmed tortillas with beef. Using a slotted spoon, spoon pepper-onion mixture over beef. If desired, top with chile peppers. Roll up.

NUTRITION FACTS PER SERVING: 282 calories, 8 g total fat (3 g saturated fat), 40 mg cholesterol, 179 mg sodium, 30 g carbohydrate, 0 g fiber, 20 g protein.

Flank Steak
with Corn Salsa

SERVE THIS THREE-INGREDIENT SALSA WITH PORK OR CHICKEN TOO.

1 8¾-ounce can whole kernel corn, drained	**2** tablespoons cracked black pepper
¾ cup salsa verde	**1** tablespoon Worcestershire sauce
1 medium tomato, chopped	**1** teaspoon ground cumin
1 1¼- to 1½-pound beef flank steak	Whole green chile peppers (optional)
¾ cup bottled Italian salad dressing	

EXCHANGES: ¹/₂ Starch, 3 Lean Meat **Prep:** 15 minutes
Marinate: 6 to 24 hours **Broil:** 15 minutes **Makes:** 6 servings

1 For salsa, in medium bowl combine corn, salsa verde, and tomato. Cover and refrigerate for at least 6 hours or up to 24 hours.

2 Meanwhile, trim fat from beef. Score both sides of beef in a diamond pattern by making shallow diagonal cuts at 1-inch intervals. Place beef in a self-sealing plastic bag set in a shallow dish.

3 For marinade, in a small bowl combine salad dressing, black pepper, Worcestershire sauce, and cumin. Pour over beef; close bag. Marinate in the refrigerator for at least 6 hours or up to 24 hours, turning bag occasionally. Drain beef, discarding marinade.

4 Place meat on the unheated rack of a broiler pan. Broil 4 to 5 inches from the heat for 15 to 18 minutes until medium doneness (160°), turning once.

5 To serve, thinly slice beef diagonally across the grain. Serve with salsa. If desired, garnish with chile peppers.

NUTRITION FACTS PER SERVING: 197 calories, 10 g total fat (0 g saturated fat), 44 mg cholesterol, 313 mg sodium, 9 g carbohydrate, 2 g fiber, 19 g protein.

Flank Steak
with Bean Relish

**THIS SIZZLING STEAK TOPPED WITH LIP-SMACKING RELISH
WILL WIN YOUR FAMILY'S WHOLE-HEARTED APPROVAL.**

½ of a 15-ounce can (¾ cup)
    black beans, drained and
    rinsed
⅔ cup corn relish
¼ cup halved and thinly sliced
    radishes
1 small fresh jalapeño
    pepper, seeded and finely
    chopped*

2 teaspoons lime juice
¼ teaspoon ground cumin
1 12-ounce beef flank steak
   Salt
   Black pepper
   Fresh rosemary sprigs
    (optional)

EXCHANGES: 1½ Starch, 2 Lean Meat **Prep:** 15 minutes
Chill: 30 minutes to 4 hours **Broil:** 15 minutes **Makes:** 4 servings

1 For relish, in a small bowl combine black beans, corn relish, radishes, jalapeño pepper, lime juice, and cumin. Cover; chill in the refrigerator for at least 30 minutes or up to 4 hours.

2 Trim fat from steak. Score both sides of steak in a diamond pattern by making shallow diagonal cuts at 1-inch intervals. Sprinkle with salt and black pepper. Place steak on the unheated rack of a broiler pan. Broil 4 to 5 inches from heat for 15 to 18 minutes for medium doneness (160°), turning once. [Or, place steak on the rack of an uncovered grill. Grill directly over medium coals for 17 to 21 minutes or until medium doneness (160°), turning once.]

3 To serve, thinly slice steak diagonally across the grain. Serve with relish. If desired, garnish with rosemary sprigs.

NUTRITION FACTS PER SERVING: 221 calories, 6 g total fat (3 g saturated fat), 40 mg cholesterol, 488 mg sodium, 22 g carbohydrate, 3 g fiber, 20 g protein.

*Note: Because chile peppers, such as jalapeños, contain volatile oils that can burn your skin and eyes, avoid direct contact with them as much as possible. When working with chile peppers, wear plastic or rubber gloves. If your bare hands do touch the chile peppers, wash your hands and nails well with soap and warm water.

Garlic Steaks with
Nectarine-Onion Relish

**SERVE PLENTY OF CRUSTY BREAD WITH THIS FRUIT-TOPPED BEEF
TO CAPTURE ALL OF THE DELICIOUS JUICES. (PICTURED ON PAGE 103.)**

4 boneless beef top loin
steaks, cut 1 inch thick
(1½ to 2 pounds total)
6 cloves garlic, thinly sliced
Salt
Pepper
1 teaspoon olive oil

2 medium onions, coarsely
chopped
2 tablespoons cider vinegar
1 tablespoon honey
1 medium nectarine, chopped
2 teaspoons snipped fresh
applemint, pineapplemint,
or spearmint

Fresh applemint,
pineapplemint, or
spearmint sprigs
(optional)

EXCHANGES: 1 Vegetable, ½ Fruit, 4 Lean Meat **Prep:** 25 minutes
Chill: 30 minutes to 8 hours **Grill:** 11 minutes **Makes:** 4 servings

1 Trim fat from steaks. With the point of a paring knife, make small slits in steaks. Insert half of the garlic into slits. Wrap steaks in plastic wrap; chill in the refrigerator for at least 30 minutes or up to 8 hours.

2 Meanwhile, for relish, in a large nonstick skillet heat oil. Cook onions and remaining garlic in hot oil over medium heat about 10 minutes or until onions are a deep golden color, stirring occasionally. Stir in vinegar and honey. Stir in nectarine and the snipped mint; heat through.

3 Sprinkle steaks with salt and pepper. Place steaks on the rack of an uncovered grill. Grill directly over medium coals until desired doneness, turning once. [Allow 11 to 15 minutes for medium-rare (145°) or 14 to 18 minutes for medium doneness (160°).] Serve the relish with steaks. If desired, garnish with mint sprigs.

NUTRITION FACTS PER SERVING: 272 calories, 9 g total fat (3 g saturated fat), 97 mg cholesterol, 108 mg sodium, 13 g carbohydrate, 1 g fiber, 34 g protein.

Ginger Beef Stir-Fry

ROUND STEAK AND SPRING VEGETABLES TEAM UP FOR A CAN'T-MISS MEAL FROM A WOK.

8 ounces beef top round steak
½ cup lower-sodium beef broth
3 tablespoons reduced-sodium soy sauce
2½ teaspoons cornstarch
1 teaspoon sugar

½ teaspoon grated fresh ginger
Nonstick cooking spray
12 ounces asparagus spears, trimmed and cut into 1-inch pieces
1½ cups sliced fresh mushrooms

1 cup small broccoli flowerets
4 green onions, bias-sliced into 1-inch pieces
1 tablespoon cooking oil
2 cups hot cooked rice

EXCHANGES: 1¹/₂ Starch, 1¹/₂ Vegetable, 2 Lean Meat **Start to Finish:** 45 minutes **Makes:** 4 servings

1 Trim fat from beef. Partially freeze beef; thinly slice across the grain into bite-size strips. Set aside. For the sauce, in a small bowl stir together the broth, soy sauce, cornstarch, sugar, and ginger. Set aside.

2 Coat an unheated wok or large skillet with nonstick cooking spray. Preheat over medium-high heat. Add asparagus, mushrooms, broccoli, and green onions. Stir-fry for 3 to 4 minutes or until vegetables are crisp-tender. Remove from wok or skillet.

3 Carefully add the oil to wok or skillet. Add beef; stir-fry for 2 to 3 minutes or until desired doneness. Push the beef from center of wok or skillet. Stir sauce; add to the wok or skillet. Cook and stir until thickened and bubbly.

4 Return vegetables to wok or skillet. Stir all ingredients together to coat with sauce; heat through. Serve with hot cooked rice.

NUTRITION FACTS PER SERVING: 252 calories, 6 g total fat (1 g saturated fat), 24 mg cholesterol, 532 mg sodium, 30 g carbohydrate, 2 g fiber, 20 g protein.

Hot Asian
Beef and Pasta

SOMETIMES LABELED "PEKING SAUCE," HOISIN SAUCE IS A TASTY BLEND OF SOYBEANS, GARLIC, CHILE PEPPERS, AND SPICES.

12 ounces boneless beef top sirloin steak, cut 1 inch thick

4 ounces dried spaghetti or vermicelli, broken, or rotini

¼ cup orange juice

2 tablespoons hoisin sauce

1 tablespoon reduced-sodium soy sauce

½ teaspoon toasted sesame oil

⅛ teaspoon ground red pepper

Nonstick cooking spray

1 clove garlic, minced

10 ounces fresh asparagus, trimmed and cut into 1-inch pieces

1 medium carrot, cut into thin strips

1 small red onion, cut into wedges

EXCHANGES: 2 Starch, 1 Vegetable, 2¹/₂ Lean Meat **Start to Finish:** 45 minutes **Makes:** 4 servings

1 Trim fat from beef. Partially freeze beef; thinly slice across the grain into bite-size strips. Set aside.

2 Cook pasta according to package directions, except omit any oil or salt. Drain pasta. Cover; keep warm.

3 Meanwhile, for sauce, stir together orange juice, hoisin sauce, soy sauce, toasted sesame oil, and ground red pepper. Set aside.

4 Coat an unheated wok or 12-inch skillet with nonstick cooking spray. Preheat over medium-high heat until a drop of water sizzles. Add garlic; stir-fry for 15 seconds. Add asparagus and carrot; stir-fry for 1 minute. Add onion; stir-fry for 2 to 3 minutes more or until vegetables are crisp-tender. Remove vegetables from wok or skillet.

5 Add beef to wok or skillet. Stir-fry about 3 minutes or until desired doneness. Return vegetables to wok or skillet. Drizzle sauce over all. Toss to coat all ingredients. Heat through. Serve over pasta.

NUTRITION FACTS PER SERVING: 331 calories, 9 g total fat (3 g saturated fat), 57 mg cholesterol, 353 mg sodium, 35 g carbohydrate, 2 g fiber, 26 g protein.

Spicy Beef
and Bean Burgers

**THE BEANS IN THESE SPUNKY BURGERS ADD
PROTEIN AND FIBER WITHOUT ADDING FAT OR CHOLESTEROL.**

1 slightly beaten egg white	**¼** cup finely chopped celery	**1** pound lean ground beef
½ of a 15-ounce can (¾ cup) pinto beans, drained and mashed	**1** tablespoon canned diced green chili peppers or 1 teaspoon chopped canned jalapeño peppers	**8** lettuce leaves
¼ cup soft whole wheat bread crumbs	**⅛** teaspoon garlic powder	**4** 7-inch flour tortillas, halved
		1 cup bottled salsa

EXCHANGES: 1 Starch, 2 Lean Meat **Prep:** 15 minutes **Broil:** 10 minutes **Makes:** 8 servings

1 In a large bowl combine egg white, beans, bread crumbs, celery, chili peppers, and garlic powder. Add ground beef; mix well.

2 Shape meat mixture into eight ½-inch-thick oval patties. Place the patties on the unheated rack of a broiler pan. Broil 4 to 5 inches from the heat for 10 to 12 minutes or until done (160°),* turning once.

3 To serve, place a lettuce leaf and a burger in the center of each tortilla half. Top each burger with 1 tablespoon of the salsa. Bring ends of each tortilla up and over burger. Top each with another 1 tablespoon of the remaining salsa.

NUTRITION FACTS PER SERVING: 185 calories, 8 g total fat (2 g saturated fat), 36 mg cholesterol, 339 mg sodium, 16 g carbohydrate, 2 g fiber, 14 g protein.

*Note: The internal color of a ground meat patty is not a reliable doneness indicator. A beef, veal, lamb, or pork patty cooked to 160°, regardless of color, is safe. Use an instant-read thermometer to check the internal temperature. To measure the doneness of a patty, insert an instant-read thermometer through the side of the patty to a depth of 2 to 3 inches.

Veal Scaloppine
with Marsala Skillet

IF VEAL ISN'T AVAILABLE, CHICKEN IS AN ECONOMICAL SUBSTITUTE.

- **1½** cups fresh mushrooms (such as crimini, porcini, morel, shiitake, or button), quartered, halved, or sliced
- **2** green onions, sliced (¼ cup)

- **4** teaspoons butter or margarine
- **8** ounces veal leg round steak or veal sirloin steak or 2 medium skinless, boneless chicken breast halves (about 8 ounces total)

- **⅛** teaspoon salt
- **⅛** teaspoon pepper
- **⅓** cup dry Marsala or dry sherry
- **¼** cup chicken broth
- **1** tablespoon snipped fresh parsley

EXCHANGES: 1 Vegetable, 3½ Very Lean Meat, 3 Fat **Start to Finish:** 15 minutes **Makes:** 2 servings

1 In a 12-inch skillet cook mushrooms and green onions in 2 teaspoons of the butter or margarine for 4 to 5 minutes or until tender. Remove from skillet, reserving drippings. Set aside.

2 Meanwhile, cut veal into 2 serving-size pieces. Place each piece of veal or chicken between 2 sheets of plastic wrap. Working from center to edges, pound lightly with the flat side of a meat mallet to about ⅛-inch thickness. Remove the plastic wrap.

3 Sprinkle veal or chicken with salt and pepper. In the same skillet cook veal or chicken in the remaining butter or margarine over medium-high heat about 2 minutes or until cooked through, turning once. Transfer to dinner plates. Keep warm.

4 Add Marsala or sherry and broth to drippings in skillet. Bring to boiling. Boil gently, uncovered, about 1 minute, scraping up any browned bits. Return mushroom mixture to skillet; add parsley. Heat through. To serve, spoon the mushroom mixture over meat.

NUTRITION FACTS PER SERVING: 283 calories, 12 g total fat (6 g saturated fat), 112 mg cholesterol, 384 mg sodium, 6 g carbohydrate, 1 g fiber, 27 g protein.

Cranberry
Pork Chops

YOU DON'T HAVE TO SAVE CRANBERRIES JUST FOR THE HOLIDAYS. HERE THEY BRING
OUT THE BEST IN PORK CHOPS FOR A DISH THAT TASTES INCREDIBLE ANYTIME.

½ teaspoon pepper
¼ teaspoon celery salt
4 boneless pork loin chops
   (about 12 ounces total)
2 teaspoons cooking oil
1 large onion, thinly sliced
   and separated into rings
2 tablespoons water
¾ cup cranberries

¼ cup sugar
3 tablespoons water
2 tablespoons frozen orange
   juice concentrate, thawed
1 teaspoon finely shredded
   orange peel
½ teaspoon ground sage
¼ teaspoon salt

EXCHANGES: 1¹/₂ Fruit, 2 Lean Meat **Start to Finish:** 30 minutes **Makes:** 4 servings

1 In a small bowl stir together pepper and celery salt; rub onto both sides of chops. In a medium skillet heat oil over medium-high heat. Cook pork chops and onion rings in hot oil until chops are browned, turning once. Carefully add the 2 tablespoons water to skillet. Cover and cook over medium heat for 15 to 20 minutes more or until juices run clear (160°). Transfer chops to serving plate; keep warm. Remove onions from juices with a slotted spoon. Set aside.

2 Meanwhile, for the sauce, in a medium saucepan combine cranberries, sugar, the 3 tablespoons water, the orange juice concentrate, orange peel, sage, and salt. Cook and stir over medium heat about 10 minutes or until the cranberry skins pop and mixture thickens. Stir in the onions; heat through. Serve sauce with pork chops.

NUTRITION FACTS PER SERVING: 209 calories, 8 g total fat (2 g saturated fat), 38 mg cholesterol, 264 mg sodium, 22 g carbohydrate, 2 g fiber, 13 g protein.

Herb-Stuffed
Pork Tenderloin

BECAUSE PORK TENDERLOINS ARE USUALLY BETWEEN 12 AND 16 OUNCES, YOU'LL PROBABLY NEED TO BUY TWO FOR THIS RECIPE. FREEZE THE EXTRA TO USE LATER.

18 ounces pork tenderloin	**3** tablespoons fine dry bread crumbs
2 tablespoons Dijon-style mustard	**1** slightly beaten egg white
1½ cups shredded romaine	**2** teaspoons olive oil or cooking oil
½ cup assorted snipped fresh herbs (such as sage, thyme, rosemary, dill, basil, marjoram, chervil, and/or savory)	Pepper
	1 recipe Mustard Sauce
	Snipped fresh chives (optional)

EXCHANGES: 3 Lean Meat **Prep:** 30 minutes **Roast:** 50 minutes **Makes:** 6 servings

1 Trim any fat from tenderloin. Using a sharp knife, make a lengthwise cut down the center of the tenderloin, cutting to, but not through, the other side. Spread the tenderloin flat. Place tenderloin between 2 sheets of plastic wrap and pound meat lightly with the flat side of a meat mallet to about a 13x8-inch rectangle. (If necessary, use a portion of a second tenderloin to make 18 ounces. Overlap and pound the pieces to make a single rectangle.) Fold in the narrow ends as necessary to make an even rectangle. Spread mustard evenly over tenderloin.

2 In a medium bowl stir together romaine, assorted herbs, bread crumbs, and egg white. Spoon evenly over tenderloin. Roll up into a spiral, beginning with a narrow end. Tie with 100%-cotton kitchen string, first at center, then at 1-inch intervals toward ends.

3 Place roll on a rack in a shallow roasting pan. Brush oil over roll. Sprinkle with pepper. Roast, uncovered, in a 375° oven for 50 or 60 minutes or until pork is tender and juices run clear (160°). Transfer to a warm platter. Remove strings; keep warm while preparing Mustard Sauce. To serve, cut tenderloin into 12 slices. Spoon some of the Mustard Sauce over each serving. If desired, garnish with snipped chives.

Mustard Sauce: In a small saucepan combine ⅓ cup plain fat-free yogurt, 2 tablespoons fat-free mayonnaise dressing or salad dressing, 1½ to 2 teaspoons Dijon-style mustard, and 1 teaspoon honey. Cook over low heat for 2 to 3 minutes or just until heated through. Do not boil.

NUTRITION FACTS PER SERVING: 162 calories, 5 g total fat (1 g saturated fat), 61 mg cholesterol, 308 mg sodium, 6 g carbohydrate, 0 g fiber, 21 g protein.

Jamaican Pork
Chops with Melon Salsa

**ALLSPICE IS PLENTIFUL IN JAMAICA, WHICH IS WHY IT
IS A COMMON INGREDIENT IN JAMAICAN JERK SEASONING.**

1 cup chopped honeydew
   melon
1 cup chopped cantaloupe
1 tablespoon snipped fresh
   mint
1 tablespoon honey
4 boneless pork top loin
   chops, cut ¾ to 1 inch
   thick

4 teaspoons purchased or
   homemade Jamaican
   jerk seasoning*
Cooked thin, lengthwise
   slices of zucchini or yellow
   summer squash (optional)
Star anise and/or fresh
   mint sprigs (optional)

EXCHANGES: 1 Fruit, 2½ Lean Meat **Prep:** 15 minutes **Grill:** 12 minutes **Makes:** 4 servings

1 For salsa, in a medium bowl combine honeydew melon, cantaloupe, snipped mint, and honey. Cover and chill in the refrigerator until ready to serve.

2 Trim fat from chops. Rub both sides of the chops with Jamaican jerk seasoning. Place chops on the rack of an uncovered grill. Grill directly over medium coals for 12 to 15 minutes or until juices run clear (160°). Serve the salsa with chops. If desired, serve over squash and garnish with star anise and/or mint sprigs.

NUTRITION FACTS PER SERVING: 189 calories, 8 g total fat (3 g saturated fat), 51 mg cholesterol, 231 mg sodium, 13 g carbohydrate, 1 g fiber, 17 g protein.

*Note: To make homemade Jamaican jerk seasoning, in a small bowl combine 1 teaspoon crushed red pepper; ½ teaspoon ground allspice; ¼ teaspoon curry powder; ¼ teaspoon coarsely ground black pepper; ⅛ teaspoon dried thyme, crushed; ⅛ teaspoon ground red pepper; and ⅛ teaspoon ground ginger.

Pork with Apple-Sour Cream Sauce

APPLE ADDS A HINT OF SWEETNESS TO THESE TENDER PORK SLICES BATHED IN A CREAMY SAGE-ACCENTED SAUCE.

12 ounces pork tenderloin Nonstick cooking spray	**¼** teaspoon dried sage, crushed	**1** 9-ounce package refrigerated spinach fettuccine or 4 ounces dried spinach fettuccine, cooked and drained
1 medium apple, cored and thinly sliced	**1** 8-ounce carton fat-free dairy sour cream	
¾ cup apple juice or apple cider	**2** tablespoons all-purpose flour	Cracked black pepper (optional)
1 small onion, chopped		
¼ teaspoon salt		

EXCHANGES: 2 Starch, ¹/₂ Milk, 1 Fruit, 2¹/₂ Very Lean Meat **Start to Finish:** 30 minutes **Makes:** 4 servings

1 Trim fat from pork. Cut pork crosswise into 4 slices. Place each slice, cut side down, between 2 sheets of plastic wrap. Lightly pound meat with the flat side of a meat mallet to ¹/₂-inch thickness.

2 Coat an unheated large skillet with nonstick cooking spray. Preheat over medium heat. Cook the pork slices, half at a time, in the skillet over medium-high heat for 3¹/₂ to 4 minutes or until juices run clear, turning once. Remove pork from skillet. Keep warm.

3 For sauce, add apple slices, apple juice, onion, salt, and sage to skillet. Bring just to boiling; reduce heat. Cover and simmer for 4 to 5 minutes or just until apple is tender. Using a slotted spoon, carefully remove apple slices and set aside. In a small bowl stir together sour cream and flour. Add sour cream mixture to skillet. Cook and stir until thickened and bubbly. Cook and stir for 1 minute more. Arrange pork and apple slices over fettuccine. Spoon sauce over pork, apple slices, and pasta. If desired, sprinkle with pepper.

NUTRITION FACTS PER SERVING: 373 calories, 4 g total fat (1 g saturated fat), 60 mg cholesterol, 231 mg sodium, 54 g carbohydrate, 1 g fiber, 28 g protein.

Saucy Apple
Pork Roast

TEAM PEPPER-CRUSTED PORK WITH APPLE WEDGES IN A SWEET MUSTARD SAUCE AND WHAT DO YOU GET? A MAIN DISH THAT'S HARD TO RESIST.

1 3½- to 4-pound boneless pork top loin roast (double loin, tied)
3 cloves garlic, cut into thin slices
1 teaspoon coarse salt or regular salt
1 teaspoon dried rosemary, crushed
½ teaspoon coarsely ground black pepper
3 medium apples, cored and cut into wedges
¼ cup packed brown sugar
¼ cup apple juice or apple cider
2 tablespoons lemon juice
2 teaspoons dry mustard

EXCHANGES: ½ Fruit, 2 Lean Meat **Prep:** 15 minutes
Roast: 1¾ hours **Stand:** 10 minutes **Makes:** 10 to 12 servings

1 Trim fat from pork. Cut small slits (about ½ inch wide and 1 inch deep) in pork; insert a piece of garlic in each slit. For rub, in a small bowl combine salt, rosemary, and black pepper. Rub into pork. Place pork on a rack in a shallow roasting pan. Insert a meat thermometer into center of a loin. Roast, uncovered, in a 325° oven for 1¼ to 1¾ hours or until the meat thermometer registers 145°. Spoon off any fat in roasting pan.

2 In a large bowl combine the apples, brown sugar, apple juice, lemon juice, and dry mustard. Spoon the apple mixture around pork. Roast, uncovered, for 30 to 45 minutes more or until meat thermometer registers 155°.

3 Transfer pork to a serving platter. Cover pork with foil; let stand for 10 minutes before slicing. (The internal temperature will rise about 5° during standing.)

4 Remove the rack from the roasting pan. Stir the apple wedges into the pan juices. Serve with pork.

NUTRITION FACTS PER SERVING: 237 calories, 11 g total fat (4 g saturated fat), 72 mg cholesterol, 271 mg sodium, 12 g carbohydrate, 1 g fiber, 23 g protein.

Pork Chops
with Italian Vegetables

THIS MINUTE-MINDING RECIPE ALLOWS YOU TO COOK
THE VEGETABLES IN A SKILLET WHILE THE CHOPS BROIL.

---

1 tablespoon frozen orange
   juice concentrate, thawed
1 clove garlic, minced
⅛ teaspoon black pepper
4 boneless pork loin chops,
   cut ½ inch thick (about
   1¼ pounds total)
   Nonstick cooking spray

2 medium zucchini and/or
   yellow summer squash,
   cut into thin strips
1 small red or green sweet
   pepper, cut into strips
1 small onion, sliced
2 teaspoons snipped fresh
   basil or ¾ teaspoon dried
   basil, crushed

1 teaspoon snipped fresh
   oregano or ½ teaspoon
   dried oregano, crushed
⅛ teaspoon salt
8 cherry tomatoes, halved
   Fresh basil sprigs (optional)

EXCHANGES: 2 Vegetable, 3 Lean Meat **Start to Finish:** 30 minutes **Makes:** 4 servings

1 In a small bowl combine orange juice concentrate, garlic, and black pepper. Set aside.

2 Trim fat from chops. Place chops on the unheated rack of a broiler pan. Broil 4 to 5 inches from the heat for 4 minutes. Brush with orange juice mixture. Turn and broil about 4 minutes more or until juices run clear. Brush with remaining orange juice mixture.

3 Meanwhile, coat an unheated large skillet with nonstick cooking spray. Add zucchini, sweet pepper, onion, dried basil (if using), dried oregano (if using), and salt. Cook and stir over medium-high heat about 4 minutes or until vegetables are crisp-tender. Stir in tomato halves, snipped fresh basil (if using), and fresh oregano (if using). Reduce heat; cover and cook for 1 minute more. Serve with chops. If desired, garnish with basil sprigs.

NUTRITION FACTS PER SERVING: 201 calories, 8 g total fat (3 g saturated fat), 71 mg cholesterol, 138 mg sodium, 8 g carbohydrate, 2 g fiber, 24 g protein.

Teriyaki
Beef Soup

FOR THOSE EVENINGS WHEN TIME IS AT A PREMIUM, ASSEMBLE THE INGREDIENTS THE NIGHT BEFORE, AND QUICKLY SIMMER THEM JUST BEFORE SERVING.

8 ounces boneless beef sirloin steak
2 teaspoons olive oil
1 large shallot, cut into thin rings
4 cups water
1 cup apple juice or apple cider

2 carrots, cut into bite-size strips (1 cup)
⅓ cup long grain rice
1 tablespoon grated fresh ginger
1 teaspoon instant beef bouillon granules
3 cloves garlic, minced

2 cups broccoli flowerets
1 to 2 tablespoons reduced-sodium teriyaki sauce
1 tablespoon dry sherry (optional)

EXCHANGES: ¹/₂ Starch, 2 Vegetable, ¹/₂ Fruit, 1 Lean Meat, ¹/₂ Fat
Prep: 20 minutes **Cook:** 18 minutes **Makes:** 5 servings

1 Trim fat from beef. Cut beef into bite-size strips. In a large saucepan heat oil over medium-high heat. Cook and stir beef and shallot in hot oil for 2 to 3 minutes or until beef is brown. Remove beef mixture with a slotted spoon. Set aside.

2 In same saucepan combine water, apple juice, carrots, uncooked rice, ginger, bouillon granules, and garlic. Bring to boiling; reduce heat. Cover and simmer about 15 minutes or until carrots are tender.

3 Stir in the broccoli and beef mixture. Cover and simmer for 3 minutes. Stir in the teriyaki sauce and, if desired, the dry sherry.

NUTRITION FACTS PER SERVING: 197 calories, 6 g total fat (2 g saturated fat), 30 mg cholesterol, 382 mg sodium, 22 g carbohydrate, 2 g fiber, 13 g protein.

Chunky Chipotle
Pork Chili

**YOU'LL SAY "WOW" WHEN YOU DISCOVER YOU CAN
COOK UP THIS HEARTY PORK STEW IN JUST MINUTES.**

2 teaspoons cooking oil
1 small onion, chopped
4 cloves garlic, minced
12 ounces pork tenderloin, cut
into ¾-inch cubes
2 teaspoons chili powder
2 teaspoons ground cumin
1 medium yellow or red sweet
pepper, cut into ½-inch
pieces

1 cup water
½ cup bottled picante sauce
or salsa
1 to 2 tablespoons finely
chopped chipotle peppers
in adobo sauce
1 teaspoon instant
low-sodium beef
bouillon granules

1 16-ounce low-sodium pinto
beans, rinsed and drained
½ cup fat-free or light dairy
sour cream
¼ cup snipped fresh cilantro

EXCHANGES: 1 Starch, 2 Vegetable, 2¹/₂ Very Lean Meat, ¹/₂ Fat
Start to Finish: 25 minutes **Makes:** 4 servings

1 In a large saucepan heat oil over medium-high heat. Cook onion and garlic in hot oil about 3 minutes or until tender.

2 Toss pork with chili powder and cumin; add to saucepan. Cook and stir about 3 minutes or until pork is browned.

3 Add sweet pepper, water, picante sauce or salsa, chipotle peppers, and bouillon granules. Bring to boiling; reduce heat. Simmer, uncovered, about 5 minutes or until pork is cooked through. Add beans; heat through. Ladle into bowls; top with sour cream and cilantro.

NUTRITION FACTS PER SERVING: 249 calories, 5 g total fat (1 g saturated fat), 53 mg cholesterol, 474 mg sodium, 26 g carbohydrate, 5 g fiber, 24 g protein.

Pork and
Eggplant Stew

**WITH ONLY 138 CALORIES PER SERVING, SPRINKLING ON
THE OPTIONAL FETA CHEESE IS A FLAVORFUL ADDITION THAT'S WELL WORTH IT.**

Nonstick cooking spray
8 ounces lean boneless pork,
cut into ¾-inch cubes
1 large onion, sliced and
separated into rings
1 clove garlic, minced
1 small eggplant, peeled and
cubed (4 cups)

1 14½-ounce can low-sodium
tomatoes, cut up
1 medium green sweet
pepper, cut into strips
1 5½-ounce can low-sodium
vegetable juice
1 teaspoon dried oregano,
crushed

1 teaspoon dried basil,
crushed
¼ teaspoon salt
¼ teaspoon black pepper
2 tablespoons snipped fresh
parsley
¼ cup crumbled feta cheese
(optional)

EXCHANGES: 3 Vegetable, 1 Lean Meat **Prep:** 30 minutes **Cook:** 10 minutes **Makes:** 4 servings

1 Coat a Dutch oven with nonstick cooking spray. Preheat over medium heat. Add pork, onion, and garlic; cook until pork is browned and onion is tender.

2 Stir in eggplant, undrained tomatoes, green sweet pepper, vegetable juice, oregano, basil, salt, and black pepper.

3 Bring to boiling; reduce heat. Cover and simmer for 10 to 15 minutes or until vegetables are tender. Stir in parsley. Divide the stew among 4 soup bowls. If desired, sprinkle each serving with crumbled feta cheese.

NUTRITION FACTS PER SERVING: 138 calories, 4 g total fat (1 g saturated fat), 26 mg cholesterol, 180 mg sodium, 15 g carbohydrate, 4 g fiber, 10 g protein.

Beef and
Basil Salad

ADDING LIVELY HERBS AND SPICES TO A SALAD, SUCH AS THIS ONE, MEANS
YOU CAN SKIP SOME OF THE FAT AND SALT AND STILL HAVE A FIRST-RATE DISH.

1 large tomato, chopped
½ of a medium yellow sweet
    pepper, cut into thin strips
    (½ cup)
¼ cup snipped fresh basil
2 tablespoons balsamic
    vinegar
1 tablespoon olive oil
1 clove garlic, minced

8 ounces beef flank steak or
    beef top loin steak
6 cups torn mixed salad
    greens
    Nonstick cooking spray
1 clove garlic, minced
¼ teaspoon black pepper
⅛ teaspoon salt

EXCHANGES: 1½ Vegetable, 1½ Lean Meat **Prep:** 25 minutes
Chill: 4 to 24 hours **Cook:** 5 minutes **Makes:** 4 servings

1 In a medium bowl stir together the tomato, sweet pepper, and basil. In a screw-top jar combine vinegar, oil, and 1 clove garlic. Cover and shake well. Pour over vegetable mixture, tossing to coat. Cover and chill in the refrigerator for at least 4 hours or up to 24 hours.

2 Meanwhile, partially freeze beef. Trim any fat from meat. Cut into thin bite-size strips. Set aside. Arrange mixed greens on 4 dinner plates.

3 Coat a large skillet with nonstick cooking spray. Add beef and 1 clove garlic. Cook and stir over medium-high heat for 2 to 3 minutes or to desired doneness. Sprinkle with black pepper and salt. Stir in tomato mixture. Heat through. Top greens on each plate with some of the beef-vegetable mixture. Serve immediately.

NUTRITION FACTS PER SERVING: 153 calories, 8 g total fat (2 g saturated fat), 27 mg cholesterol, 114 mg sodium, 8 g carbohydrate, 2 g fiber, 13 g protein.

Fajita
Beef Salad

LIME DOES DOUBLE DUTY IN THIS RECIPE—IT'S IN BOTH THE MARINADE AND
THE DRESSING. ITS TART FLAVOR ENHANCES THE HONEY-KISSED DRESSING.

½ teaspoon finely shredded
   lime peel
⅓ cup lime juice
3 tablespoons water
4 teaspoons olive oil
¼ cup chopped onion
1 clove garlic, minced

12 ounces beef flank steak
3 tablespoons water
2 tablespoons powdered
   fruit pectin
2 tablespoons honey
6 cups torn mixed salad
   greens

2 small red and/or yellow
   tomatoes, cut into wedges
1 small avocado, halved,
   seeded, peeled, and
   chopped (optional)

EXCHANGES: 2 Vegetable, ¹/₂ Fruit, 2 Lean Meat, ¹/₂ Fat **Prep:** 35 minutes
Marinate: 24 hours **Grill:** 17 minutes **Makes:** 4 servings

1 In a screw-top jar combine the lime peel, lime juice, 3 tablespoons water, and the olive oil. Cover and shake well. Pour half of the lime juice mixture into a small bowl; stir in onion and garlic. Reserve remaining lime juice mixture.

2 Score both sides of steak in a diamond pattern by making shallow diagonal cuts at 1-inch intervals. Place steak in a self-sealing plastic bag set in a shallow dish. Pour the lime juice-onion mixture over the steak. Close bag. Marinate in the refrigerator for 24 hours, turning occasionally.

3 Meanwhile, for dressing, in a small bowl gradually stir 3 tablespoons water into fruit pectin; stir in reserved lime juice mixture and honey. Cover and chill in the refrigerator for 24 hours.

4 Drain steak, discarding marinade. Place steak on the rack of an uncovered grill. Grill directly over medium coals for 17 to 21 minutes or until medium doneness (160°), turning once. [Or, place steak on the unheated rack of a broiler pan. Broil 4 to 5 inches from the heat for 15 to 18 minutes or until medium doneness (160°), turning once.]

5 To serve, thinly slice beef across grain. Arrange the greens, tomatoes, and, if desired, the avocado on 4 dinner plates. Top with sliced beef. Drizzle each serving with about 2 tablespoons of the dressing.

NUTRITION FACTS PER SERVING: 224 calories, 9 g total fat (3 g saturated fat), 40 mg cholesterol, 72 mg sodium, 20 g carbohydrate, 2 g fiber, 18 g protein.

Pork and
Fruit Salad

HONEY MUSTARD, PINEAPPLE JUICE, AND FRESH GINGER MAKE FOR A MAGNIFICENT
MAYONNAISE DRESSING TO DRIZZLE ON THIS FRUIT AND PORK MEDLEY.

¼ cup fat-free mayonnaise
    dressing or salad dressing
¼ cup unsweetened pineapple
    juice or orange juice
1 tablespoon honey mustard
½ teaspoon grated fresh
    ginger
12 ounces pork tenderloin
2 tablespoons honey mustard

6 cups torn fresh spinach
    and/or romaine
2 cups sliced pears, apples,
    nectarines, and/or peeled
    peaches
12 small clusters champagne
    grapes
Coarsely ground black
    pepper (optional)

EXCHANGES: 1½ Vegetable, 1 Fruit, 2½ Lean Meat **Prep:** 15 minutes **Roast:** 25 minutes
Stand: 5 minutes **Makes:** 4 servings

1 For dressing, in a small bowl stir together the mayonnaise dressing or salad dressing, pineapple juice or orange juice, the 1 tablespoon honey mustard, and the ginger. Cover and chill in the refrigerator until serving time.

2 Trim fat from tenderloin. Place in a shallow roasting pan. Insert a meat thermometer into center of tenderloin. Roast, uncovered, in a 425° oven for 20 minutes.

3 Spoon the 2 tablespoons honey mustard over the tenderloin. Roast for 5 to 10 minutes more or until thermometer registers 160°. Cover meat loosely with foil and let stand for 5 minutes before slicing.

4 Meanwhile, arrange spinach or romaine, fruit slices, and grapes on 4 dinner plates. Thinly slice pork tenderloin. Add pork slices to plates. Stir dressing. Drizzle dressing over salads. If desired, sprinkle with pepper.

NUTRITION FACTS PER SERVING: 228 calories, 4 g total fat (1 g saturated fat), 60 mg cholesterol, 442 mg sodium, 27 g carbohydrate, 5 g fiber, 22 g protein.

Pork and
Mango Salad

**MANGO AND PORK ARE A WINNING COMBINATION.
HERE MANGO STARS IN BOTH THE DRESSING AND THE SALAD.**

3 tablespoons mango chutney	**1** tablespoon water	**1** medium mango, peeled,
2 tablespoons white wine	**8** ounces pork tenderloin	seeded, and sliced, or
vinegar or rice vinegar	Nonstick cooking spray	2 medium nectarines,
1 tablespoon Dijon-style	**6** cups torn mixed salad	sliced
mustard or brown mustard	greens	**2** tablespoons snipped fresh
1 clove garlic, minced	**½** of an 8-ounce can sliced	chives
⅛ teaspoon pepper	water chestnuts, drained	Fresh chives (optional)
1 tablespoon olive oil		

EXCHANGES: 1 Vegetable, 1 Fruit, 2 Lean Meat **Start to Finish:** 30 minutes **Makes:** 4 servings

1 For vinaigrette, in a blender container or food processor bowl combine chutney, vinegar, mustard, garlic, and pepper. Cover and blend or process until smooth. In a small bowl combine oil and the water. With blender or food processor running, add oil mixture in a thin steady stream to chutney mixture; blend or process for 15 seconds more.

2 Trim any fat from the pork; cut pork into ¼-inch slices. Coat a large skillet with nonstick cooking spray. Preheat the skillet over medium-high heat. Add pork; cook for 3 to 4 minutes or until pork is cooked through, turning once. Remove pork from skillet; keep warm.

3 In a large bowl toss together the salad greens and water chestnuts. Pour about half of the vinaigrette over the greens mixture. Toss to coat.

4 To serve, divide greens mixture among 4 dinner plates. Arrange mango or nectarine slices and pork on the greens mixture. Drizzle each serving with about 1 tablespoon of the remaining vinaigrette. Sprinkle with the snipped chives. If desired, garnish with whole chives.

NUTRITION FACTS PER SERVING: 192 calories, 6 g total fat (1 g saturated fat), 40 mg cholesterol, 137 mg sodium, 21 g carbohydrate, 2 g fiber, 14 g protein.

Fish & Seafood

CHOOSE FROM FISH, SHRIMP, CRAB, OR SCALLOPS. YOU'LL FIND DELECTABLE IDEAS FOR THEM ALL IN THIS CHAPTER.

Spicy Red Snapper with
Mango Salsa **page 158**

Citrus Sole

WITH LESS THAN 200 CALORIES AND ONLY 5 GRAMS OF FAT PER
SERVING, THIS SUNNY DISH IS AS GOOD FOR YOU AS IT IS SATISFYING.

2 fresh or frozen sole or whitefish fillets (about 6 ounces total)	Pepper
	1 teaspoon butter or margarine, melted
1 orange	⅛ teaspoon salt
1 cup kashi pilaf mix or long grain rice	⅛ teaspoon paprika
	Dash pepper
1 cup chopped fresh broccoli	**1** recipe Citrus Sauce
Salt	Fresh herb sprigs (optional)

EXCHANGES: ¹/₂ Fruit, 2 Lean Meat, 1 Fat **Start to Finish:** 40 minutes **Makes:** 2 servings

1 Thaw fish, if frozen. Rinse fish; pat dry with paper towels. Set aside. Peel orange, trim off bitter white pith, and slice into 4 slices. Set aside.

2 For pilaf, cook pilaf mix or rice according to package directions, except stir in broccoli for the last 5 minutes of cooking. Season to taste with salt and pepper.

3 Meanwhile, grease the unheated rack of a broiler pan. Place fish on rack, tucking under any thin edges. Combine butter or margarine, the ¹/₈ teaspoon salt, the paprika, and the dash pepper; brush over fish. Arrange orange slices around fish on broiler pan. Broil about 4 inches from the heat for 4 to 6 minutes or just until fish flakes easily when tested with a fork and fruit is heated through. Serve fish and orange slices with pilaf and Citrus Sauce. If desired, garnish with fresh herb sprigs.

Citrus Sauce: Combine ¹/₄ cup light dairy sour cream, 1 tablespoon orange marmalade, and ¹/₈ teaspoon dried thyme or herbes de Provence, crushed. Cover; chill in the refrigerator until serving time.

NUTRITION FACTS PER SERVING: 183 calories, 5 g total fat (3 g saturated fat), 49 mg cholesterol, 254 mg sodium, 19 g carbohydrate, 2 g fiber, 17 g protein.

Fish with Cherry Relish

THE CHERRY RELISH BECOMES MORE FLAVORFUL IF YOU
ASSEMBLE IT A DAY AHEAD, REFRIGERATE IT, AND REHEAT TO SERVE.

4 fresh or frozen swordfish steaks,* cut ¾-inch thick (about 1¼ pounds total)
½ cup dried tart cherries, snipped
2 tablespoons raspberry vinegar, balsamic vinegar, or white wine vinegar
1 tablespoon water

1 teaspoon olive oil
⅓ cup chopped red onion
1½ teaspoons sugar
Dash bottled hot pepper sauce
½ teaspoon dried thyme, crushed
¼ teaspoon paprika
¼ teaspoon black pepper

⅛ teaspoon onion powder
⅛ teaspoon ground red pepper
1 teaspoon olive oil
1 teaspoon raspberry vinegar, balsamic vinegar, or white wine vinegar
Nonstick cooking spray

EXCHANGES: 1 Fruit, 4 Lean Meat **Prep:** 20 minutes **Grill:** 6 minutes **Makes:** 4 servings

1 Thaw fish, if frozen. Rinse fish; pat dry with paper towels. Set aside.

2 For the relish, in a small bowl stir together the cherries, the 2 tablespoons vinegar, and the water. Set aside. In a small saucepan heat 1 teaspoon oil. Cook onion in oil until tender. Stir in cherry mixture, sugar, and hot pepper sauce. Keep warm over low heat until serving time, stirring occasionally.

3 In a small bowl stir together thyme, paprika, black pepper, onion powder, and ground red pepper. Combine 1 teaspoon oil and the 1 teaspoon vinegar. Lightly brush both sides of fish with the oil mixture. Rub the herb mixture onto both sides of the fish.

4 Coat the unheated rack of an uncovered grill with nonstick cooking spray. Place fish on the rack. Grill directly over medium coals for 6 to 9 minutes or just until fish flakes easily when tested with a fork, turning once. (Or, coat the unheated rack of a broiler pan with nonstick cooking spray. Place the fish on the rack. Broil 4 inches from the heat for 6 to 9 minutes or just until fish flakes easily when tested with a fork.) Serve with relish.

NUTRITION FACTS PER SERVING: 254 calories, 8 g total fat (2 g saturated fat), 56 mg cholesterol, 128 mg sodium, 16 g carbohydrate, 1 g fiber, 29 g protein.

*Note: If swordfish is unavailable, or if you prefer a different fish, try halibut, tuna, or any other firm-fleshed fish.

Flounder with Tomatoes and Peppers

FOR THOSE TIMES WHEN YOU'RE DINING ALONE,
REMEMBER THIS QUICK FISH AND VEGETABLE MEAL IN A SKILLET.

1 or 2 fresh or frozen flounder fillets or other thin mild-flavored fillets (5 ounces)

2 teaspoons olive oil

1 small mild green chile pepper, chopped (⅔ cup)*

⅓ cup finely chopped onion or shallot

2 small plum tomatoes, chopped (about ⅔ cup)

1 teaspoon capers, drained

3 imported black olives (such as kalamata or niçoise), pitted and sliced (optional)

⅛ teaspoon black pepper Fresh parsley sprigs (optional)

EXCHANGES: 4 Vegetable, 3 Very Lean Meat, 2 Fat **Start to Finish:** 20 minutes **Makes:** 1 serving

1 Thaw fish, if frozen. Rinse fish; pat dry with paper towels. Set aside. In a medium skillet heat the oil over medium heat. Cook green chile pepper and onion or shallot in hot oil about 4 minutes or until tender. Add the tomatoes; cover and simmer for 5 minutes.

2 Stir in the capers and, if desired, olives. Arrange the flounder fillets on top of vegetables. Sprinkle the fish and vegetables with black pepper. Cover and simmer 4 to 6 minutes or just until the fish flakes easily when tested with a fork. Transfer to dinner plate. If desired, garnish with parsley sprigs.

NUTRITION FACTS PER SERVING: 295 calories, 11 g total fat (2 g saturated fat), 68 mg cholesterol, 219 mg sodium, 20 g carbohydrate, 4 g fiber, 30 g protein.

*Note: Because chile peppers, such as green chile peppers, contain volatile oils that can burn your skin and eyes, avoid direct contact with them as much as possible. When working with chile peppers, wear plastic or rubber gloves. If your bare hands do touch the chile peppers, wash your hands and nails well with soap and warm water.

Seared Tuna with
Grapefruit-Orange Relish

PAN SEARING KEEPS THE TUNA STEAKS MOIST BY
SEALING IN THE JUICES AND CREATING A GOLDEN CRUST.

4 4-ounce fresh or frozen
tuna steaks, cut ¾ inch
thick
2 teaspoons sherry vinegar or
white wine vinegar
2 teaspoons soy sauce
½ teaspoon grated fresh
ginger
1 tablespoon olive oil

1 medium grapefruit, peeled
and sectioned
1 medium orange, peeled and
sectioned
2 tablespoons finely chopped
red onion
2 tablespoons snipped fresh
cilantro
2 teaspoons olive oil

Salt
Pepper
Fresh cilantro sprigs
(optional)

EXCHANGES: ¹/₂ Fruit, 4 Very Lean Meat, 2 Fat **Prep:** 20 minutes **Cook:** 6 minutes **Makes:** 4 servings

1 Thaw fish, if frozen. Rinse fish; pat dry with paper towels. Set aside. For relish, in a small bowl combine vinegar, soy sauce, and ginger. Whisk in the 1 tablespoon oil. Cut grapefruit sections into thirds and orange sections in half. Stir fruit pieces, red onion, and snipped cilantro into vinegar mixture. Set aside.

2 In large skillet heat the 2 teaspoons oil over medium-high heat. Add fish and cook for 6 to 9 minutes or just until fish flakes easily when tested with a fork, turning once. Sprinkle with salt and pepper. Serve the fish with relish. If desired, garnish with cilantro sprigs.

NUTRITION FACTS PER SERVING: 256 calories, 12 g total fat (2 g saturated fat), 47 mg cholesterol, 287 mg sodium, 7 g carbohydrate, 1 g fiber, 29 g protein.

Halibut with
Creamy Dijon Sauce

THESE DELICATE FISH STEAKS ARE BASTED WITH AN HERB SAUCE AS THEY COOK;
THEN THEY'RE TOPPED WITH A TANGY THYME AND MUSTARD COMBINATION.

4 fresh or frozen halibut or
    sea bass steaks, cut
    1 inch thick (about
    1½ pounds total)
1 tablespoon butter or
    margarine, melted
¼ teaspoon onion salt
¼ teaspoon dried marjoram,
    crushed

¼ teaspoon dried thyme,
    crushed
½ cup dairy sour cream
1 tablespoon all-purpose flour
1 tablespoon Dijon-style
    mustard
⅛ teaspoon salt
⅛ teaspoon pepper
⅛ teaspoon dried thyme,
    crushed

½ cup reduced-sodium
    chicken or vegetable broth
4 cups shredded spinach
    (5 ounces)
1 medium carrot, shredded
    (½ cup)
    Lemon wedges (optional)

EXCHANGES: 1 Vegetable, 5 Very Lean Meat, 2 Fat **Prep:** 20 minutes **Broil:** 8 minutes **Makes:** 4 servings

1 Thaw fish, if frozen. Rinse fish; pat dry with paper towels. Set aside.

2 For basting sauce, combine butter or margarine, onion salt, marjoram, and the ¼ teaspoon thyme.

3 Place fish steaks on the unheated rack of a broiler pan. Brush with basting sauce. Broil 4 inches from the heat for 8 to 12 minutes or just until fish flakes easily when tested with a fork, turning and brushing once with the remaining basting sauce halfway through broiling. (Or, grease the unheated rack of an uncovered grill. Place fish on rack. Grill directly over medium coals for 8 to 12 minutes or just until fish flakes easily with a fork, turning and brushing once with the remaining basting sauce halfway through grilling.)

4 Meanwhile, for mustard sauce, in a small saucepan stir together the sour cream, flour, mustard, salt, pepper, and the ⅛ teaspoon thyme. Add chicken or vegetable broth, stirring until well mixed. Cook and stir over medium heat until thickened and bubbly. Cook and stir for 1 minute more. Keep warm.

5 Toss together spinach and carrot. Divide the spinach mixture among 4 dinner plates. Arrange fish on spinach mixture. Top with mustard sauce. If desired, garnish with lemon wedges.

NUTRITION FACTS PER SERVING: 289 calories, 12 g total fat (5 g saturated fat), 72 mg cholesterol, 435 mg sodium, 5 g carbohydrate, 3 g fiber, 38 g protein.

Herb-Buttered Fish Steaks

SMALL FISH STEAKS ARE SOMETIMES HARD TO FIND. IF YOU CAN'T GET SMALL
ONES, BUY TWO LARGE STEAKS AND CUT THEM IN HALF JUST BEFORE SERVING.

4 small fresh or frozen
   halibut, salmon, shark, or
   swordfish steaks, cut
   1 inch thick (about
   1 pound total)
2 tablespoons butter or
   margarine, softened
1 teaspoon finely shredded
   lime peel or lemon peel

1 teaspoon lime juice or
   lemon juice
1 teaspoon snipped fresh
   tarragon or rosemary or
   ¼ teaspoon dried
   tarragon or rosemary,
   crushed
1 teaspoon butter or
   margarine, melted

EXCHANGES: 3¹/₂ Very Lean Meat, 1¹/₂ Fat **Prep:** 10 minutes **Broil:** 8 minutes **Makes:** 4 servings

1 Thaw fish, if frozen. Rinse fish; pat dry with paper towels. For herb butter, in a small bowl stir together the 2 tablespoons butter or margarine, the lime peel or lemon peel, lime juice or lemon juice, and tarragon or rosemary. Set aside.

2 Lightly grease the unheated rack of a broiler pan. Place fish on broiler pan. Brush with the 1 teaspoon butter or margarine. Broil 4 inches from the heat for 8 to 12 minutes or just until fish flakes easily when tested with a fork, turning once. To serve, top with herb butter.

NUTRITION FACTS PER SERVING: 184 calories, 9 g total fat (2 g saturated fat), 36 mg cholesterol, 140 mg sodium, 0 g carbohydrate, 0 g fiber, 24 g protein.

Spicy Red Snapper with Mango Salsa

BRING THE BOLD FLAVORS OF THE CARIBBEAN TO YOUR TABLE WITH
THIS TROPICAL TREATMENT OF RED SNAPPER. (PHOTO ON PAGE 145.)

1 pound fresh or frozen red
   snapper fillets
1 tablespoon lime juice
1 tablespoon water
1 teaspoon paprika
½ teaspoon salt
¼ teaspoon ground ginger
¼ teaspoon ground allspice
¼ teaspoon black pepper

1 recipe Mango Salsa
1 medium lime, cut into
   wedges (optional)
Fresh cilantro or parsley
   sprigs (optional)
Fresh Scotch bonnet
   peppers (optional)

EXCHANGES: 1 Fruit, 2½ Very Lean Meat, 2 Fat **Start to Finish:** 30 minutes **Makes:** 4 servings

1 Thaw fish, if frozen. Cut into 4 serving-size pieces. Rinse fish and pat dry with paper towels. Measure thickness of fish. In a small bowl combine lime juice and water; brush onto fish. In another small bowl combine paprika, salt, ginger, allspice, and black pepper; rub onto fish.

2 Arrange the fish in a shallow baking pan. Bake, uncovered, in a 450° oven just until fish flakes easily when tested with a fork. (Allow 4 to 6 minutes for each ½ inch of thickness.)

3 To serve, brush the fish with pan juices. Serve with Mango Salsa. If desired, garnish with lime wedges, cilantro or parsley sprigs, and Scotch bonnet peppers.

Mango Salsa: In a medium bowl combine 1 mango, peeled, seeded, and chopped (about 1½ cups); 1 medium red sweet pepper, seeded and finely chopped; ¼ cup thinly sliced green onions; 1 Scotch bonnet or hot green chile pepper, seeded and finely chopped*; 3 tablespoons olive oil; ½ teaspoon finely shredded lime peel; 2 tablespoons lime juice; 1 tablespoon vinegar; ¼ teaspoon salt; and ¼ teaspoon black pepper. Makes about 2 cups.

NUTRITION FACTS PER SERVING: 222 calories, 11 g total fat (2 g saturated fat), 28 mg cholesterol, 437 mg sodium, 15 g carbohydrate, 3 g fiber, 17 g protein.

*Note: Because chile peppers, such as Scotch bonnet peppers or green chile peppers, contain volatile oils that can burn your skin and eyes, avoid direct contact with them as much as possible. When working with chile peppers, wear plastic or rubber gloves. If your bare hands do touch the chile peppers, wash your hands and nails well with soap and warm water.

Spicy Broiled Shark Steaks

ORANGE JUICE, CHILI SAUCE, BASIL, AND GINGER ADD UP TO A FIRST-RATE
MARINADE FOR THE FULL-FLAVORED SHARK OR SWORDFISH STEAKS.

1 pound fresh or frozen shark
 or swordfish steaks, cut
 ¾ inch thick
2 green onions, thinly sliced
 (¼ cup)
2 tablespoons orange juice
2 tablespoons chili sauce

1 tablespoon snipped fresh
 basil or 1 teaspoon dried
 basil, crushed
1 tablespoon finely chopped
 fresh ginger
1 tablespoon reduced-sodium
 soy sauce

Several dashes hot chili oil
Nonstick cooking spray
Orange slices (optional)
Fresh chives (optional)

EXCHANGES: 3 Lean Meat **Prep:** 15 minutes **Marinate:** 30 minutes **Broil:** 10 minutes **Makes:** 4 servings

1 Thaw fish, if frozen. Cut into 4 serving-size portions. Rinse fish; pat dry with paper towels. For marinade, in a shallow bowl combine the green onions, orange juice, chili sauce, basil, ginger, soy sauce, and chili oil. Add the fish, turning to coat with marinade. Cover and marinate in the refrigerator for 30 minutes.

2 Coat the unheated rack of a broiler pan with nonstick cooking spray. Drain fish, reserving marinade. Place fish on rack. Broil 4 inches from the heat for 5 minutes. Using a wide spatula, carefully turn fish over. Brush with the reserved marinade. Broil for 5 to 7 minutes more or just until fish flakes easily when tested with a fork. If desired, serve fish on top of orange slices and garnish with chives.

NUTRITION FACTS PER SERVING: 160 calories, 5 g total fat (1 g saturated fat), 45 mg cholesterol, 342 mg sodium, 3 g carbohydrate, 0 g fiber, 23 g protein.

Shark with
Nectarine Salsa

IF SHARK ISN'T AVAILABLE AT YOUR LOCAL FISH COUNTER, ORANGE
ROUGHY, WITH ITS MILD FLAVOR AND FIRM FLESH, IS A GREAT ALTERNATIVE.

1 1-pound fresh or frozen
shark or orange roughy
fillet, about 1 inch thick
1 medium ripe nectarine, cut
into ½-inch pieces
1 small cucumber, seeded
and cut into ½-inch
pieces

1 ripe kiwi fruit, peeled and
cut into ½-inch pieces
2 green onions, thinly sliced
(¼ cup)
3 tablespoons orange juice
1 tablespoon white wine
vinegar
1 teaspoon olive oil

½ teaspoon freshly ground
black pepper

EXCHANGES: ½ Vegetable, ½ Fruit, 3 Very Lean Meat **Prep:** 30 minutes **Grill:** 8 minutes **Makes:** 4 servings

1 Thaw fish, if frozen. Rinse fish; pat dry with paper towels. Set aside. For salsa, in a medium bowl combine nectarine, cucumber, kiwi fruit, green onions, orange juice, and vinegar. Cover and chill in the refrigerator until ready to serve.

2 Rub oil over both sides of fish and sprinkle with black pepper. Grease wire grill basket well. Place fish in grill basket, tucking under any thin edges. Place grill basket on the rack of an uncovered grill. Grill directly over medium coals for 8 to 12 minutes or just until fish flakes easily when tested with a fork, turning basket once.

3 To serve, cut fish into 4 serving-size pieces. Spoon the salsa over fish.

NUTRITION FACTS PER SERVING: 158 calories, 3 g total fat (1 g saturated fat), 60 mg cholesterol, 94 mg sodium, 10 g carbohydrate, 1 g fiber, 22 g protein.

Mustard-Dill Fish Fillets

LAYERING LEMON SLICES UNDER THE FISH HELPS CREATE A
NATURAL BAKING RACK SO THE FISH DOESN'T SIT IN ITS OWN JUICES.

---

4 fresh or frozen skinless fish
fillets, about ½ inch thick
(about 1 pound total)
4 13×10-inch sheets
parchment paper or
aluminum foil
1 lemon, thinly sliced

2 tablespoons snipped fresh
dill or 1 teaspoon dried
dillweed
½ teaspoon lemon-pepper
seasoning
1 tablespoon capers, drained

EXCHANGES: 1½ Lean Meat **Prep:** 15 minutes **Bake:** 12 minutes **Makes:** 4 servings

---

1 Thaw fish, if frozen. Rinse fish; pat dry with paper towels. Fold each sheet of parchment paper or foil in half crosswise. Cut into a heart shape with the fold running vertically down the center. Open each heart to lie flat.

2 Arrange lemon slices in the center of one side of each heart. Place fish fillets over lemon slices. Sprinkle evenly with dill and lemon-pepper seasoning. Top with capers.

3 Fold the paper or foil over the fish. Beginning at the top of each heart, make a series of tight, overlapping folds to seal. Bake in a 400° oven about 12 minutes or just until fish flakes easily when tested with a fork.

NUTRITION FACTS PER SERVING: 85 calories, 1 g total fat (0 g saturated fat), 43 mg cholesterol, 235 mg sodium, 1 g carbohydrate, 0 g fiber, 18 g protein.

Grilled Rosemary Trout with Lemon Butter

THIS SIMPLE FISH RECIPE BOASTS A TIMELESS
SEASONING COMBINATION OF BUTTER, LEMON, AND ROSEMARY.

2 fresh or frozen rainbow
trout, pan dressed* and
boned (8 to 10 ounces
each)
4 teaspoons butter, softened
1 tablespoon finely chopped
shallot or onion
1 teaspoon finely shredded
lemon peel

Salt
Coarsely ground black
pepper
1 tablespoon snipped fresh
rosemary
1 tablespoon lemon juice
2 teaspoons olive oil
2 medium tomatoes, halved
crosswise

EXCHANGES: 1 Vegetable, 3 Very Lean Meat, 1¹/₂ Fat **Prep:** 15 minutes **Grill:** 6 minutes **Makes:** 4 servings

1 Thaw fish, if frozen. Rinse fish; pat dry with paper towels. Set aside. In a small bowl stir together the butter, half of the shallot or onion, and the lemon peel. Sprinkle with salt and black pepper. Set aside.

2 Spread each fish open, skin side down. Rub remaining shallot or onion and the rosemary onto fish; sprinkle with additional salt and black pepper. Drizzle with lemon juice and oil.

3 Grease a 12-inch cast-iron skillet.** Arrange hot coals in bottom of an uncovered grill. Place prepared skillet directly on coals; preheat skillet. Place fish, skin sides down, in hot skillet. Grill for 6 to 8 minutes or just until fish flakes easily when tested with a fork. Meanwhile, place the tomatoes, cut sides up, in skillet next to fish. Dot each with ¹/₄ teaspoon of the butter mixture. Grill about 5 minutes or until tomatoes are heated through.

4 Remove skillet from the grill. Cut each fish in half lengthwise. In a small saucepan melt the remaining butter mixture; serve with fish and tomatoes.

NUTRITION FACTS PER SERVING: 206 calories, 10 g total fat (3 g saturated fat), 75 mg cholesterol, 109 mg sodium, 4 g carbohydrate, 1 g fiber, 24 g protein.

***Note:** A pan-dressed fish has had the scales and internal organs removed; often the head, fins, and tail also have been removed.

****Note:** If you prefer to avoid using a skillet, place the fish, then the tomatoes on a greased rack of an uncovered grill directly over medium coals. Grill as directed.

Salmon with Fruit Salsa

PERFECT FOR A MEAL ON A HOT SUMMER DAY, THIS FLAVORFUL
BROILED FISH DISH HAS ONLY 123 CALORIES PER SERVING.

14 to 16 ounces fresh or frozen salmon or halibut steaks, cut 1 inch thick

¾ cup chopped fresh strawberries or chopped, peeled peaches or nectarines

⅓ cup chopped, peeled kiwi fruit or fresh apricots

1 tablespoon snipped fresh cilantro

1 tablespoon orange juice or apple juice

1 fresh jalapeño pepper, seeded and chopped*

1 teaspoon olive oil or cooking oil

⅛ teaspoon lemon-pepper seasoning
Nonstick cooking spray
Fresh cilantro sprigs (optional)

EXCHANGES: ½ Fruit, 2 Lean Meat **Prep:** 15 minutes **Broil:** 8 minutes **Makes:** 4 servings

1 Thaw fish, if frozen. Cut into 4 serving-size pieces. Rinse fish; pat dry with paper towels. For salsa, in a bowl stir together strawberries, peaches, or nectarines; kiwi fruit or apricots; the snipped cilantro; the orange juice or apple juice; and jalapeño pepper. Set aside.

2 Brush both sides of the fish pieces with oil. Sprinkle with lemon-pepper seasoning. Coat the unheated rack of a broiler pan with nonstick cooking spray. Place fish on rack. Broil 4 inches from heat for 8 to 12 minutes or just until fish flakes easily when tested with a fork, turning once. (Or, coat the unheated rack of an uncovered grill with nonstick cooking spray. Place fish on rack. Grill directly over medium-hot coals for 8 to 12 minutes or just until fish flakes easily when tested with a fork, turning once.) Serve with salsa. If desired, garnish with cilantro sprigs.

NUTRITION FACTS PER SERVING: 123 calories, 5 g total fat (1 g saturated fat), 18 mg cholesterol, 95 mg sodium, 5 g carbohydrate, 1 g fiber, 15 g protein.

*Note: Because chile peppers, such as jalapeños, contain volatile oils that can burn your skin and eyes, avoid direct contact with them as much as possible. When working with chile peppers, wear plastic or rubber gloves. If your bare hands do touch the chile peppers, wash your hands and nails well with soap and warm water.

Salmon with Wilted Greens

A WARM SOY SAUCE AND ORANGE DRESSING DELICATELY COATS
THE FRESH-TASTING SALMON, GREENS, AND ORANGE SECTIONS.

4 fresh or frozen salmon
steaks, cut ¾ inch thick
(about 1 pound total)
3 tablespoons orange juice
concentrate
3 tablespoons water
2 tablespoons reduced-
sodium soy sauce
1 tablespoon honey

2 teaspoons cooking oil
1 teaspoon toasted
sesame oil
½ teaspoon grated fresh
ginger or ¼ teaspoon
ground ginger
6 cups torn mixed greens*
1 small red sweet pepper, cut
into thin bite-size strips

1 medium orange, peeled and
sectioned
Orange peel strips
(optional)

EXCHANGES: 1½ Vegetable, ½ Fruit, 3½ Lean Meat **Prep:** 25 minutes **Broil:** 6 minutes **Makes:** 4 servings

1 Thaw fish, if frozen. Rinse fish; pat dry with paper towels. Set aside. For dressing, in a small bowl combine orange juice concentrate, the water, soy sauce, honey, cooking oil, toasted sesame oil, and ginger.

2 Grease the unheated rack of a broiler pan. Place fish on rack. Broil 4 inches from the heat for 3 minutes. Using a wide spatula, carefully turn fish. (Or, grease the unheated rack of an uncovered grill. Place fish on rack. Grill directly over medium coals for 3 minutes. Using a wide spatula, carefully turn fish.) Brush with 1 tablespoon of the dressing. Broil or grill for 3 to 6 minutes more or just until fish flakes easily when tested with a fork. Remove fish. Cover and keep warm.

3 Place the greens in a large salad bowl. In a large skillet bring the remaining dressing to boiling. Add red pepper strips. Remove from heat. Pour over greens, tossing to coat.

4 To serve, divide greens mixture among 4 dinner plates. Arrange the orange sections and fish on top of greens. If desired, garnish with orange peel strips.

NUTRITION FACTS PER SERVING: 255 calories, 9 g total fat (2 g saturated fat), 31 mg cholesterol, 406 mg sodium, 15 g carbohydrate, 27 g protein.

*Note: Use a combination of fresh spinach, Swiss chard, radicchio, mustard greens, beet greens, and/or collard greens.

Parmesan Baked Fish

THIS FIVE-INGREDIENT DISH IS QUICK TO FIX AND DELICIOUS TO EAT.

4 4-ounce fresh or frozen
skinless salmon or other
firm fish fillets, about
1 inch thick
Nonstick cooking spray
¼ cup light mayonnaise
dressing or salad dressing
2 tablespoons grated
Parmesan cheese

1 tablespoon snipped fresh
chives or sliced green
onion
1 teaspoon white wine
Worcestershire sauce
Fresh chives (optional)

EXCHANGES: 2¹/₂ Lean Meat, ¹/₂ Fat **Prep:** 15 minutes **Bake:** 8 minutes **Makes:** 4 servings

1 Thaw fish, if frozen. Rinse fish; pat dry with paper towels. Coat a 2-quart square or rectangular baking dish with nonstick cooking spray. Set aside.

2 In a small bowl stir together mayonnaise dressing or salad dressing, Parmesan cheese, snipped chives or sliced green onion, and Worcestershire sauce. Spread the mayonnaise mixture over fish fillets; place in the baking dish.

3 Bake, uncovered, in a 450° oven for 8 to 12 minutes or just until fish flakes easily when tested with a fork. If desired, garnish with whole chives.

NUTRITION FACTS PER SERVING: 169 calories, 10 g total fat (2 g saturated fat), 23 mg cholesterol, 247 mg sodium, 1 g carbohydrate, 0 g fiber, 18 g protein.

Salmon Fillets
Bathed in Garlic

KEEP THE MEAL SIMPLE BY ADDING A VEGETABLE SIDE DISH
AND YOUR FAVORITE FAT-FREE ICE CREAM FOR DESSERT.

6 4-ounce fresh or frozen
skinless salmon fillets,
about 1 inch thick
Coarse salt
Black pepper
¼ cup snipped fresh flat-leaf
parsley
¼ cup reduced-sodium
chicken broth

¼ cup dry white wine
1 tablespoon olive oil
4 large cloves garlic, minced
½ teaspoon crushed
red pepper

EXCHANGES: 3¹/₂ Very Lean Meat, 1 Fat **Prep:** 15 minutes **Bake:** 8 minutes **Makes:** 6 servings

1 Thaw fish, if frozen. Rinse fish and pat dry with paper towels. Sprinkle both sides of fish with salt and black pepper. Set aside.

2 In a small bowl combine parsley, broth, wine, oil, garlic, and crushed red pepper.

3 Place fish, flat sides down, in a single layer in a 2-quart rectangular baking dish. Pour parsley mixture evenly over fish.

4 Bake, uncovered, in a 450° oven for 8 to 12 minutes or just until the fish flakes easily when tested with a fork.

NUTRITION FACTS PER SERVING: 163 calories, 6 g total fat (1 g saturated fat), 59 mg cholesterol, 201 mg sodium, 1 g carbohydrate, 0 g fiber, 23 g protein.

Citrus-Herb Salmon Fillets

BOOST THE CITRUS FLAVOR OF THE BROILED SALMON
FILLETS BY SERVING THEM WITH TANGERINE OR ORANGE SLICES.

1¼ pounds fresh or frozen salmon fillet, about 1 inch thick	2 teaspoons finely shredded orange peel
Cooking oil or nonstick cooking spray	2 teaspoons finely shredded lemon peel
¼ cup packed fresh basil, cut into thin strips	⅓ cup orange juice
2 teaspoons snipped fresh tarragon	1 tablespoon lemon juice
	2 teaspoons soy sauce

EXCHANGES: 4½ Lean Meat **Prep:** 15 minutes **Marinate:** 20 minutes **Broil:** 4 minutes **Makes:** 4 servings

1 Thaw fish, if frozen. Rinse fish; pat dry with paper towels. Measure thickness of fish. Set aside. Lightly coat the unheated rack of a broiler pan with oil or nonstick cooking spray. Set aside. In a small bowl combine basil, tarragon, orange peel, and lemon peel. Set aside.

2 For sauce, in a small saucepan combine orange juice, lemon juice, and soy sauce. Set aside half of the sauce. Place remaining sauce in a self-sealing plastic bag set in a shallow dish. Place fish in bag; close bag. Turn to coat fish. Marinate in the refrigerator for 20 minutes, turning bag occasionally.

3 Remove fish from marinade; discard marinade. Place fish on the unheated rack of broiler pan. Broil 4 inches from the heat just until fish flakes easily when tested with a fork. (Allow 4 to 6 minutes for each ½ inch thickness.) Using a wide spatula, carefully turn fish halfway through broiling time.

4 Meanwhile, heat reserved sauce until heated through. To serve, spoon warmed sauce over salmon and sprinkle with basil mixture.

NUTRITION FACTS PER SERVING: 251 calories, 12 g total fat (2 g saturated fat), 87 mg cholesterol, 220 mg sodium, 3 g carbohydrate, 0 g fiber, 31 g protein.

Garlicky Shrimp and Olives

NO TIME TO PEEL AND DEVEIN SHRIMP? PICK UP 4 OUNCES OF PEELED, DEVEINED SHRIMP AT YOUR LOCAL FISH MARKET OR THE SUPERMARKET'S FISH COUNTER.

6 ounces fresh or frozen medium shrimp in shells
¼ cup diced pimiento (one 2-ounce jar)
2 tablespoons dry sherry or orange juice
1 tablespoon orange juice

1 tablespoon snipped fresh parsley
5 pitted ripe olives, halved
2 cloves garlic, minced
1 teaspoon capers, drained
1 teaspoon tomato paste
Dash coarsely ground black pepper

Hot cooked fusilli or other pasta (optional)
Fresh parsley sprigs (optional)

EXCHANGES: ¹/₂ Vegetable, 1 Lean Meat, ¹/₂ Fat **Start to Finish:** 25 minutes **Makes:** 2 servings

1 Thaw shrimp, if frozen. Peel and devein shrimp, leaving tails intact. Rinse shrimp; pat dry with paper towels. Set aside.

2 In a medium skillet combine pimiento, sherry or orange juice, the 1 tablespoon orange juice, snipped parsley, olives, garlic, capers, tomato paste, and black pepper. Bring to boiling. Add shrimp. Cook and stir for 2 to 4 minutes or until shrimp turn opaque. Remove from heat. If desired, serve over cooked pasta and garnish with parsley sprigs.

NUTRITION FACTS PER SERVING: 101 calories, 2 g total fat (0 g saturated fat), 98 mg cholesterol, 198 mg sodium, 6 g carbohydrate, 1 g fiber, 11 g protein.

Shrimp and Mushrooms in Almond Sauce

CINNAMON AND ALMONDS ARE DELIGHTFUL ACCENTS
FOR THE SHRIMP AND MUSHROOMS IN THIS ELEGANT ENTRÉE.

12 ounces fresh or frozen medium shrimp in shells	**½** teaspoon olive oil	**2** to 3 tablespoons ground blanched almonds
½ cup dry white wine	**1** small onion, thinly sliced	Salt
1 tablespoon all-purpose flour	**2** large cloves garlic, minced	Pepper
1 teaspoon olive oil	**1** medium tomato, seeded and chopped	
1½ cups sliced assorted mushrooms (such as button, shiitake, oyster, portobello, and/or crimini)	**1** cup clam juice	
	½ teaspoon dried thyme, crushed	
	¼ teaspoon ground cinnamon	
	1 bay leaf	

EXCHANGES: 1½ Vegetable, 2 Very Lean Meat, 1 Fat **Start to Finish:** 1 hour **Makes:** 4 servings

1 Thaw shrimp, if frozen. Peel and devein shrimp, leaving tails intact. Rinse shrimp; pat dry with paper towels. In a medium bowl combine shrimp and wine. Marinate in the refrigerator for 30 minutes. Drain the shrimp, reserving the wine. Toss shrimp with flour. Set aside.

2 Lightly coat a nonstick skillet with the 1 teaspoon oil. Add mushrooms; cook and stir over medium heat for 3 to 5 minutes or until mushrooms are just tender. Transfer mushrooms to a medium bowl.

3 Add shrimp to skillet; cook and stir over medium heat for 2 to 3 minutes or until the shrimp turn opaque. Transfer shrimp to the bowl with mushrooms.

4 Add the ½ teaspoon oil to skillet. Cook and stir onion and garlic in oil just until tender. Stir in tomato and reserved wine, scraping any browned bits of vegetables from bottom of pan with a wooden spoon. Bring mixture to boiling. Add the clam juice, thyme, cinnamon, and bay leaf; bring to boiling. Reduce heat and boil gently, uncovered, for 10 minutes, stirring occasionally.

5 Return shrimp and mushrooms to skillet. Add almonds. Heat over low heat just until shrimp and mushrooms are warm. Discard bay leaf. Season to taste with salt and pepper.

NUTRITION FACTS PER SERVING: 162 calories, 6 g total fat (1 g saturated fat), 97 mg cholesterol, 277 mg sodium, 8 g carbohydrate, 2 g fiber, 16 g protein.

Creole-Style Grits

SAVORING THE SHRIMP, GRITS, AND CREOLE SEASONING IN
THIS DISH IS LIKE TAKING A CULINARY TRIP TO THE FRENCH QUARTER.

1 pound fresh or frozen
  medium shrimp
½ cup quick-cooking yellow grits
1 tablespoon olive oil
12 ounces fresh asparagus,
  trimmed and bias-sliced
  into 2-inch pieces

1 medium red sweet pepper,
  cut into ½-inch squares
½ cup chopped onion
2 cloves garlic, minced
2 tablespoons all-purpose
  flour

2 teaspoons salt-free
  Creole seasoning
¾ cup chicken broth

EXCHANGES: 1 Starch, 1 Vegetable, 2¹/₂ Very Lean Meat, ¹/₂ Fat **Start to Finish:** 35 minutes **Makes:** 4 servings

1 Thaw shrimp, if frozen. Peel and devein shrimp, leaving tails intact. Rinse shrimp; pat dry with paper towels.

2 Prepare grits according to package directions. Cover and keep warm.

3 Meanwhile, in a large skillet heat oil. Cook asparagus, sweet pepper, onion, and garlic in hot oil for 4 to 5 minutes or just until vegetables are tender.

4 Stir flour and Creole seasoning into vegetable mixture. Add broth. Cook and stir until mixture begins to bubble; reduce heat. Stir in shrimp. Cover and cook for 1 to 3 minutes or until shrimp turn opaque, stirring once. Serve shrimp mixture over grits.

NUTRITION FACTS PER SERVING: 243 calories, 6 g total fat (1 g saturated fat), 129 mg cholesterol, 323 mg sodium, 25 g carbohydrate, 2 g fiber, 22 g protein.

Grilled Shrimp with Papaya Salsa

YOU CAN TELL IF A PAPAYA IS RIPE BY PRESSING IT.
IF IT YIELDS TO GENTLE PRESSURE, IT'S READY TO USE.

1½ pounds fresh or frozen large shrimp in shells
1 tablespoon butter or margarine, melted
¼ teaspoon salt
¼ teaspoon ground cumin
¼ teaspoon white pepper
⅛ teaspoon ground red pepper

1 small papaya and/or mango, peeled, seeded, and coarsely chopped (about 1⅓ cups)
⅓ cup chopped red sweet pepper
⅓ cup chopped peeled jicama
1 fresh serrano pepper, finely chopped*

2 tablespoons pineapple juice or orange juice
1 tablespoon snipped fresh cilantro or parsley
Nonstick cooking spray

EXCHANGES: 1½ Lean Meat, ½ Fat **Prep:** 30 minutes **Grill:** 6 minutes **Makes:** 6 servings

1 Thaw shrimp, if frozen. Peel and devein shrimp, leaving tails intact. Rinse shrimp; pat dry with paper towels. In a small bowl combine butter or margarine, salt, cumin, white pepper, and ground red pepper. Drizzle over shrimp, tossing to coat.

2 For salsa, in a bowl toss together papaya or mango, sweet pepper, jicama, serrano pepper, pineapple juice or orange juice, and cilantro or parsley. Set aside.

3 Coat an unheated grill basket with nonstick cooking spray. Arrange shrimp in basket. Close basket. (Or, thread shrimp on eight 8- to 10-inch metal skewers, leaving ¼ inch space between pieces.) Place basket or skewers on rack of uncovered grill. Grill directly over medium coals for 6 to 9 minutes or until shrimp turn opaque, turning once. Remove shrimp from basket or skewers. Serve with salsa.

NUTRITION FACTS PER SERVING: 102 calories, 3 g total fat (1 g saturated fat), 136 mg cholesterol, 259 mg sodium, 5 g carbohydrate, 0 g fiber, 14 g protein.

*Note: Because chile peppers, such as serranos, contain volatile oils that can burn your skin and eyes, avoid direct contact with them as much as possible. When working with chile peppers, wear plastic or rubber gloves. If your bare hands do touch the chile peppers, wash your hands and nails well with soap and warm water.

Shrimp
Kabobs

FOR BOLDER FLAVOR, BRUSH THESE KABOBS WITH A FIERY BARBECUE SAUCE.

1 pound fresh or frozen medium to large shrimp in shells

1 small green or red sweet pepper, cut into 16 pieces

¼ of a medium fresh pineapple, cut into chunks

4 green onions, cut into 1-inch pieces

Nonstick cooking spray

¼ cup bottled barbecue sauce

Lettuce leaves (optional)

EXCHANGES: ¹/₂ Fruit, 1¹/₂ Lean Meat **Prep:** 20 minutes **Broil:** 8 minutes **Makes:** 4 servings

1 Thaw shrimp, if frozen. Peel and devein shrimp, leaving tails intact. Rinse shrimp; pat dry with paper towels. On eight 8- to-10-inch skewers alternately thread shrimp, sweet pepper pieces, pineapple chunks, and green onions.

2 Coat the unheated rack of a broiler pan with nonstick cooking spray. Place the kabobs on rack. Broil 4 inches from heat for 8 to 10 minutes or until shrimp turn opaque, turning skewers and brushing with barbecue sauce halfway through broiling. (Or, coat the unheated rack of an uncovered grill with nonstick cooking spray. Place kabobs on rack. Grill the skewers directly over medium coals for 6 to 8 minutes or until shrimp are opaque, turning and brushing with barbecue sauce halfway through grilling.) Discard any remaining barbecue sauce. If desired, serve on lettuce leaves.

NUTRITION FACTS PER SERVING: 101 calories, 1 g total fat (0 g saturated fat), 131 mg cholesterol, 277 mg sodium, 8 g carbohydrate, 1 g fiber, 15 g protein.

Chunky Vegetable-Cod Soup

A TRIO OF HERBS RAISES THIS DELECTABLE FISH STEW A NOTCH ABOVE THE REST.

1 pound fresh or frozen skinless cod fillets or steaks	**3½** cups reduced-sodium chicken broth or vegetable broth	**1** teaspoon snipped fresh thyme
½ cup chopped red sweet pepper	**1** cup frozen cut green beans	**½** teaspoon snipped fresh rosemary
¼ cup chopped onion	**1** cup coarsely chopped cabbage	**¼** teaspoon black pepper
1 tablespoon butter or margarine	**½** cup sliced carrot	Lemon wedges (optional)
	1 teaspoon snipped fresh basil	

EXCHANGES: 1½ Vegetable, 3 Very Lean Meat, ½ Fat **Start to Finish:** 30 minutes **Makes:** 4 servings

1 Thaw fish, if frozen. Rinse fish; pat dry with paper towels. Cut into 1-inch pieces. In a large saucepan or Dutch oven cook red pepper and onion in hot butter or margarine until tender.

2 Stir in the broth, green beans, cabbage, carrot, basil, thyme, rosemary, and black pepper. Bring to boiling; reduce heat. Cover and simmer for 8 to 10 minutes or until vegetables are nearly tender.

3 Stir fish into broth mixture. Return to boiling; reduce heat. Cover and simmer about 5 minutes or just until fish flakes easily when tested with a fork, stirring once. If desired, serve the fish with lemon wedges.

NUTRITION FACTS PER SERVING: 176 calories, 4 g total fat (2 g saturated fat), 62 mg cholesterol, 555 mg sodium, 8 g carbohydrate, 2 g fiber, 25 g protein.

Salmon Chowder

WHEN CHOOSING SALMON FOR THIS SOUP, LOOK FOR FILLETS
THAT HAVE A MILD AROMA AND APPEAR MOIST AND FRESHLY CUT.

1 pound fresh or frozen
  skinless salmon fillets or
  one 15-ounce can
  salmon, rinsed, drained,
  flaked, and skin and
  bones removed
1 tablespoon cooking oil
2 cups coarsely shredded
  carrots

1 cup finely chopped onion
½ cup thinly sliced celery
1½ cups water
4 cups reduced-sodium
  chicken broth
2½ cups cubed red-skinned
  potatoes (3 medium)
1 10-ounce package frozen
  whole kernel corn

1 teaspoon snipped fresh dill
  or ½ teaspoon dried
  dillweed
¼ teaspoon salt
2 cups fat-free milk
2 tablespoons cornstarch

EXCHANGES: 1 Starch, 2 Vegetable, 1 Lean Meat, ¹/₂ Fat **Start to Finish:** 45 minutes **Makes:** 8 servings

1 Thaw fish, if frozen. Rinse fresh or thawed fish; pat dry with paper towels. Set aside. In a large saucepan heat oil over medium-high heat. Cook and stir carrots, onion, and celery in hot oil about 10 minutes or until the vegetables are tender, stirring occasionally.

2 Meanwhile, to poach fresh or thawed fish, in a large skillet bring the water to boiling. Add fish. Return to boiling; reduce heat. Cover and simmer for 6 to 8 minutes or just until the fish flakes easily when tested with a fork. Remove fish from skillet, discarding poaching liquid. Flake fish into ¹/₂-inch pieces. Set aside.

3 Stir the chicken broth, potatoes, corn, dill, and salt into vegetables in saucepan. Bring to boiling; reduce heat. Cover and cook over medium-low heat about 15 minutes or until the potatoes are tender, stirring occasionally.

4 Stir together ¹/₂ cup of the milk and the cornstarch. Add milk mixture to saucepan. Stir in remaining milk. Cook and stir over medium heat until thickened and bubbly. Cook and stir for 2 minutes more. Gently stir in poached or canned fish. Heat through.

NUTRITION FACTS PER SERVING: 211 calories, 5 g total fat (1 g saturated fat), 11 mg cholesterol, 487 mg sodium, 30 g carbohydrate, 3 g fiber, 14 g protein.

Spicy Seafood Stew

YOU'LL THINK YOU'VE BEEN TRANSPORTED TO THE BAYOU WHEN
YOU SAMPLE THIS CAJUN-SEASONED SHRIMP AND FISH SENSATION.

8 ounces fresh or frozen skinless fish fillets (such as halibut, orange roughy, or sea bass)
6 ounces fresh or frozen peeled and deveined shrimp
2 teaspoons olive oil
⅔ cup chopped onion
½ cup finely chopped carrot
½ cup chopped green or red sweet pepper

2 cloves garlic, minced
1 14½-ounce can low-sodium tomatoes, cut up
1 8-ounce can low-sodium tomato sauce
1 cup reduced-sodium chicken broth
¼ cup dry red wine or reduced-sodium chicken broth
2 bay leaves

1 tablespoon snipped fresh thyme or 1 teaspoon dried thyme, crushed
½ teaspoon Cajun seasoning
¼ teaspoon ground cumin
¼ teaspoon crushed red pepper (optional)
Crackers (optional)

EXCHANGES: 3 Vegetable, 2 Lean Meat **Prep:** 15 minutes **Cook:** 25 minutes **Makes:** 4 servings

1 Thaw fish and shrimp, if frozen. Rinse fish and shrimp; pat dry with paper towels. Cut the fish into 1-inch pieces. Cover and chill fish pieces and shrimp in the refrigerator until needed.

2 In a large saucepan heat oil over medium-high heat. Cook and stir onion, carrot, sweet pepper, and garlic in hot oil until tender. Stir in the undrained tomatoes, tomato sauce, the 1 cup chicken broth, wine or additional chicken broth, bay leaves, dried thyme (if using), Cajun seasoning, cumin, and, if desired, crushed red pepper. Bring the mixture to boiling; reduce heat. Cover and simmer for 20 minutes.

3 Gently stir in the fish pieces, shrimp, and fresh thyme (if using). Cover and simmer about 5 minutes more or just until the fish flakes easily when tested with a fork and shrimp turn opaque. Discard bay leaves. If desired, serve with crackers.

NUTRITION FACTS PER SERVING: 199 calories, 5 g total fat (1 g saturated fat), 84 mg cholesterol, 341 mg sodium, 15 g carbohydrate, 3 g fiber, 22 g protein.

Zuppa di Pesce

THIS ITALIAN-STYLE FISH STEW IS OFTEN SERVED OVER CROSTINI OR TOAST.
OR IF YOU LIKE, SPRINKLE EACH SERVING WITH GARLIC-FLAVORED CROUTONS.

8 ounces fresh or frozen skinless cod or sea bass fillets
6 ounces fresh or frozen peeled and deveined shrimp
2 teaspoons olive oil
⅓ cup chopped onion
2 stalks celery, sliced
1 clove garlic, minced

1 cup reduced-sodium chicken broth
¼ cup dry white wine or reduced-sodium chicken broth
1 14½-ounce can low-sodium tomatoes, drained and cut up
1 8-ounce can low-sodium tomato sauce

1 teaspoon dried oregano, crushed
¼ teaspoon salt
⅛ teaspoon pepper
1 tablespoon snipped fresh parsley
Fresh oregano sprigs (optional)

EXCHANGES: 2 Vegetable, 2 Very Lean Meat, ¹/₂ Fat **Start to Finish:** 30 minutes **Makes:** 4 servings

1 Thaw fish and shrimp, if frozen. Rinse fish and shrimp; pat dry with paper towels. Cut fish into 1¹/₂-inch pieces. Cut shrimp in half. Cover and chill fish and shrimp in the refrigerator until needed.

2 For soup, in a large saucepan heat oil. Cook onion, celery, and garlic in hot oil until tender. Carefully stir in the 1 cup broth and wine or additional broth. Bring to boiling; reduce heat. Simmer, uncovered, for 5 minutes. Stir in the drained tomatoes, tomato sauce, oregano, salt, and pepper. Return to boiling; reduce heat. Cover and simmer for 5 minutes.

3 Gently stir in fish and shrimp. Return just to boiling; reduce heat to low. Cover and simmer for 3 to 5 minutes or just until fish flakes easily when tested with a fork and shrimp turn opaque. Stir in parsley. Ladle into serving bowls. If desired, garnish with oregano sprigs.

NUTRITION FACTS PER SERVING: 165 calories, 4 g total fat (1 g saturated fat), 87 mg cholesterol, 459 mg sodium, 12 g carbohydrate, 2 g fiber, 19 g protein.

Salmon Salad

REMINISCENT OF CAESAR SALAD, THIS DEFTLY-SEASONED COMBINATION GETS ITS CAPTIVATING FLAVOR FROM A CREAMY GARLIC AND LEMON DRESSING.

12 ounces fresh or frozen skinless salmon fillets, about 1 inch thick
2 tablespoons olive oil
5 cloves garlic, thinly sliced
2 tablespoons lemon juice
1 tablespoon Worcestershire sauce

1 tablespoon Dijon-style mustard
1 tablespoon water
½ teaspoon pepper
⅓ cup plain fat-free yogurt
Nonstick cooking spray
10 cups torn romaine
½ cup thinly sliced red onion

¼ cup freshly grated Parmesan cheese
1 cup cherry tomatoes, halved
½ cup pitted ripe olives, halved (optional)
Plain fat-free yogurt (optional)

EXCHANGES: 2 Vegetable, 2 Lean Meat, 1 Fat **Prep:** 20 minutes
Chill: 30 minutes **Broil:** 8 minutes **Makes:** 4 servings

1 Thaw fish, if frozen. Rinse fish; pat dry with paper towels. Cut fish into 4 serving-size pieces; set aside. In a small saucepan heat oil over medium-low heat. Cook and stir garlic in hot oil for 1 to 2 minutes or until garlic is lightly golden. Transfer garlic to a blender container. Add lemon juice, Worcestershire sauce, mustard, water, and pepper. Cover; blend until combined. Reserve 2 tablespoons of the garlic mixture. Set aside. Add the ¹/₃ cup yogurt to remaining garlic mixture in blender. Cover and blend until smooth. Chill in the refrigerator until serving time.

2 Brush the reserved garlic mixture evenly over fish. Cover and chill in the refrigerator for 30 minutes.

3 Coat the unheated rack of a broiler pan with nonstick cooking spray. Place the fish on the rack. Broil 4 inches from heat for 8 to 12 minutes or just until fish flakes easily when tested with a fork, turning once.

4 Meanwhile, in large bowl toss romaine, onion, and Parmesan cheese with the chilled yogurt mixture. Divide romaine mixture among 4 dinner plates. Place a fish piece on each salad. Top with tomatoes and, if desired, olives. If desired, top fish with additional yogurt.

NUTRITION FACTS PER SERVING: 234 calories, 13 g total fat (3 g saturated fat), 21 mg cholesterol, 331 mg sodium, 12 g carbohydrate, 4 g fiber, 19 g protein.

Tuna-Pasta Salad

THIS SIMPLE MAKE-AHEAD SALAD IS IDEAL FOR TOTING TO POTLUCKS.

3 ounces dried corkscrew
   macaroni (about 1 cup)
1 medium carrot, thinly sliced
½ of a medium cucumber,
   quartered lengthwise and
   sliced
½ of a medium red sweet
   pepper, chopped

2 green onions, sliced
⅓ cup bottled reduced-calorie
   creamy Italian or ranch
   salad dressing
1 6-ounce can low-sodium
   chunk light tuna, drained
   Romaine or lettuce leaves

EXCHANGES: 1 Starch, 1 Vegetable, 1 Lean Meat **Prep:** 25 minutes **Chill:** 2 to 6 hours **Makes:** 4 servings

1 Cook pasta according to package directions, except omit any oil and salt. Drain. Rinse with cold water; drain again.

2 In a large bowl toss together drained pasta, carrot, cucumber, sweet pepper, and green onions. Add salad dressing. Toss to coat. Gently stir in tuna. Cover and chill in the refrigerator for at least 2 hours or up to 6 hours.

3 Arrange romaine or lettuce on 4 dinner plates. Spoon tuna mixture over greens.

NUTRITION FACTS PER SERVING: 166 calories, 3 g total fat (0 g saturated fat), 1 mg cholesterol, 261 mg sodium, 22 g carbohydrate, 2 g fiber, 13 g protein.

Scallops and Pasta Salad

PECTIN GIVES BODY TO THE ORANGE DRESSING FOR THIS MAIN-DISH PASTA SALAD.
YOU'LL FIND PECTIN IN THE CANNING SUPPLY SECTION OF YOUR SUPERMARKET.

1 teaspoon finely shredded orange peel	**8** ounces fresh or frozen sea scallops	**½** cup coarsely chopped red onion
⅓ cup orange juice	**6** ounces dried medium shell macaroni	**½** cup thinly sliced celery
¼ cup white wine vinegar		**⅓** cup chopped red sweet pepper
2 tablespoons powdered fruit pectin	**2** cups water	
1 tablespoon sugar	**4** cups torn fresh spinach	
	1 cup frozen peas	

EXCHANGES: 2 Starch, 1 Vegetable, 1 Lean Meat **Prep:** 30 minutes **Chill:** 3 to 24 hours **Makes:** 5 servings

1 For dressing, in a small bowl stir together the orange peel, orange juice, vinegar, pectin, and sugar until smooth. Cover and chill in the refrigerator for at least 3 hours or up to 24 hours.

2 Meanwhile, thaw scallops, if frozen. Cook macaroni according to package directions; drain. Rinse with cold water; drain again.

3 Cut any large scallops in half. Rinse scallops; pat dry with paper towels. Bring the water to boiling; add scallops. Return to boiling. Simmer, uncovered, for 1 to 3 minutes or until scallops turn opaque. Drain. Rinse under cold running water.

4 For salad, in a large bowl toss together cooked macaroni, cooked scallops, spinach, peas, red onion, celery, and sweet pepper. Stir dressing; pour over salad. Toss to coat.

NUTRITION FACTS PER SERVING: 227 calories, 1 g total fat (0 g saturated fat), 14 mg cholesterol, 142 mg sodium, 42 g carbohydrate, 4 g fiber, 13 g protein.

Crab-Stuffed Tomatoes

DRAINING EXCESS JUICE FROM THE TOMATO HELPS
KEEP THE CRAB FILLING FROM BECOMING RUNNY.

4 large tomatoes
1 6-ounce package frozen
cooked crabmeat, thawed,
or a 6-ounce can
crabmeat, drained, flaked,
and cartilage removed
½ cup finely chopped celery
¼ cup fine dry bread crumbs

2 tablespoons snipped fresh
chives
1 tablespoon snipped fresh
basil or ½ teaspoon dried
basil, crushed
1 tablespoon lemon juice
1 teaspoon Dijon-style
mustard
Dash pepper

⅛ teaspoon salt
Fresh basil sprigs (optional)
Leaf lettuce (optional)
Red and/or yellow cherry
tomatoes (optional)

EXCHANGES: ¹/₂ Starch, 1 Vegetable, 1 Lean Meat **Start to Finish:** 25 minutes **Makes:** 4 servings

1 Cut off a ¹/₄-inch slice from the stem end of each large tomato. Using a spoon, scoop the pulp from each tomato into a mesh sieve, leaving a ¹/₄- to ¹/₂-inch-thick shell. Invert tomatoes; drain on paper towels. Drain tomato pulp and discard excess juice. Chop the tomato pulp.

2 In a medium bowl combine chopped tomato pulp, crabmeat, celery, bread crumbs, chives, snipped or dried basil, lemon juice, mustard, and pepper. Sprinkle salt inside tomato shells. Fill tomatoes with crab mixture. If desired, garnish with basil sprigs. If desired, serve on lettuce leaves and garnish with cherry tomatoes.

NUTRITION FACTS PER SERVING: 105 calories, 2 g total fat (0 g saturated fat), 43 mg cholesterol, 290 mg sodium, 13 g carbohydrate, 2 g fiber, 11 g protein.

Shrimp Salad

BALSAMIC VINEGAR BRINGS OUT THE NATURAL GOODNESS OF ASPARAGUS AND SHRIMP.

12 ounces fresh or frozen peeled and deveined shrimp	**1** tablespoon snipped fresh basil	**4** cups water
2 tablespoons snipped dried tomato (not oil-packed)	**2** teaspoons Dijon-style mustard	**1** clove garlic
¼ cup balsamic vinegar	**2** cloves garlic, minced	**8** ounces fresh asparagus, cut into 2-inch pieces
2 tablespoons olive oil	¼ teaspoon sugar	**6** cups torn mixed salad greens
	⅛ teaspoon pepper	**2** medium pears, thinly sliced

EXCHANGES: 2 Vegetable, ½ Fruit, 2 Lean Meat, ½ Fat **Prep:** 25 minutes **Chill:** 4 to 24 hours **Makes:** 4 servings

1 Thaw shrimp, if frozen. Rinse shrimp; pat dry with paper towels. Set aside. In a small bowl pour boiling water over snipped tomato to cover; let stand for 2 minutes. Drain.

2 For dressing, in a screw-top jar combine snipped tomato, vinegar, oil, basil, mustard, the 2 cloves garlic, the sugar, and pepper. Cover and shake well. Cover and chill in the refrigerator for up to 24 hours.

3 Meanwhile, in a large saucepan bring the water and the 1 clove garlic to boiling; add asparagus. Return to boiling. Simmer, uncovered, for 4 minutes. Add shrimp. Return to boiling. Simmer, uncovered, for 1 to 3 minutes more or until shrimp turn opaque. Drain, discarding garlic. Rinse under cold running water; drain well. Cover and chill in the refrigerator for at least 4 hours or up to 24 hours.

4 To serve, divide greens and pears among 4 dinner plates. Top with shrimp and asparagus. Shake dressing; drizzle each serving with about 2 tablespoons of the dressing.

NUTRITION FACTS PER SERVING: 221 calories, 8 g total fat (1 g saturated fat), 131 mg cholesterol, 260 mg sodium, 21 g carbohydrate, 4 g fiber, 17 g protein.

EGGS, CHEESE, BEANS, AND
VEGETABLES STAR IN THESE
GREAT-TASTING MAIN DISHES.

Meatless Meals

Streusel French Toast

DRESS UP FRENCH TOAST FOR COMPANY WITH THIS INNOVATIVE ADAPTATION
FEATURING A CRUNCHY TOPPING AND A CINNAMON AND STRAWBERRY SAUCE.

Nonstick cooking spray
¾ cup refrigerated or frozen
    egg product, thawed, or
    3 slightly beaten eggs
1 cup evaporated fat-free milk
3 tablespoons sugar
2 teaspoons vanilla
½ teaspoon ground cinnamon

¼ teaspoon ground nutmeg
6 1-inch-thick slices Italian
    bread (3 to 4 inches in
    diameter)
1 large shredded wheat
    biscuit, crushed (⅔ cup)
1 tablespoon butter or
    margarine, melted

2 cups sliced strawberries
3 tablespoons sugar, or sugar
    substitute equal to
    3 tablespoons sugar
½ teaspoon ground cinnamon

EXCHANGES: 2 Starch, ½ Milk, ½ Fruit, ½ Lean Meat **Prep:** 20 minutes
Chill: 2 to 24 hours **Bake:** 30 minutes **Makes:** 6 servings

1 Coat a 2-quart rectangular baking dish with nonstick cooking spray. Set aside. In a medium bowl beat together the egg product or eggs, evaporated milk, 3 tablespoons sugar, the vanilla, ½ teaspoon cinnamon, and the nutmeg. Arrange the bread slices in a single layer in baking dish. Pour egg mixture evenly over slices. Cover and chill in the refrigerator for at least 2 hours or up to 24 hours, turning bread slices once with a wide spatula.

2 Combine crushed biscuit and butter or margarine; sprinkle evenly over the bread slices. Bake, uncovered, in a 375° oven about 30 minutes or until lightly browned.

3 Meanwhile, in a small bowl combine the strawberries, 3 tablespoons sugar or sugar substitute, and ½ teaspoon cinnamon. Serve with French toast.

NUTRITION FACTS PER SERVING: 244 calories, 5 g total fat (2 g saturated fat), 7 mg cholesterol, 300 mg sodium, 41 g carbohydrate, 1 g fiber, 10 g protein.

Cranberry-Wheat Pancakes

FOR A COMPANY-SPECIAL BREAKFAST, TEAM THESE CRANBERRY-FILLED GRIDDLE
CAKES WITH A FRUIT COMPOTE AND YOUR FAVORITE TEA OR FLAVORED COFFEE.

1 recipe Orange Sauce	**1½** cups evaporated fat-free milk	**½** cup dried cranberries, snipped
1 cup whole wheat flour	**¼** cup refrigerated or frozen egg product, thawed	**1** teaspoon finely shredded orange peel
½ cup all-purpose flour	**2** tablespoons butter, melted	Nonstick cooking spray
1 tablespoon sugar	**1** teaspoon vanilla	
1 tablespoon baking powder		
½ teaspoon salt		

EXCHANGES: 1$^{1}/_{2}$ Starch, $^{1}/_{2}$ Milk, 1 Fruit, $^{1}/_{2}$ Fat **Prep:** 30 minutes
Cook: 4 minutes per batch **Makes:** 6 servings (12 pancakes)

1 Prepare Orange Sauce; keep warm.

2 In a large bowl combine the whole wheat flour, all-purpose flour, sugar, baking powder, and salt. Make a well in the center of mixture; set aside. In another bowl combine evaporated milk, egg product, butter, and vanilla; add all at once to flour mixture. Stir just until moistened (batter should be slightly lumpy). Fold in the cranberries and orange peel.

3 Coat an unheated griddle or heavy skillet with nonstick cooking spray. Preheat over medium-high heat. For each pancake, pour about $^{1}/_{4}$ cup of the batter onto hot griddle or skillet. Spread batter into a circle about 4 inches in diameter. Cook over medium heat about 2 minutes on each side or until pancakes are golden brown, turning to cook second sides when pancakes have bubbly surfaces and edges are slightly dry. Serve pancakes with Orange Sauce.

Orange Sauce: In a small saucepan combine 1 teaspoon finely shredded orange peel, $^{3}/_{4}$ cup orange juice, $^{1}/_{3}$ cup water, 3 packets heat-stable low-calorie sweetener or 2 tablespoons sugar, 2 tablespoons snipped dried cranberries (if desired), and 1 tablespoon cornstarch. Cook and stir over medium heat until thickened and bubbly. Cook and stir for 2 minutes more. Makes 1 cup sauce.

NUTRITION FACTS PER 2 PANCAKES WITH ABOUT 3 TABLESPOONS SAUCE: 250 calories, 5 g total fat (2 g saturated fat), 7 mg cholesterol, 500 mg sodium, 44 g carbohydrate, 4 g fiber, 10 g protein.

Tex-Mex Breakfast Pizza

TEX-MEX TAKES ON AN ITALIAN ACCENT IN THIS JALAPEÑO-SEASONED OMELET SPOONED OVER AN ITALIAN BREAD SHELL. (PICTURED ON PAGE 205.)

Nonstick cooking spray
1½ cups loose-pack frozen diced hash brown potatoes, thawed
2 green onions, sliced (¼ cup)
1 to 2 canned jalapeño peppers or canned whole green chile peppers, drained, seeded, and chopped

¼ teaspoon ground cumin
1 clove garlic, minced
1 cup refrigerated or frozen egg product, thawed
¼ cup fat-free milk
1 tablespoon snipped fresh cilantro
1 16-ounce Italian bread shell (Boboli)

½ cup shredded reduced-fat Monterey Jack cheese (2 ounces)
1 small tomato, seeded and chopped

EXCHANGES: 2 Starch, 1 Lean Meat **Prep:** 25 minutes **Bake:** 8 minutes **Makes:** 8 servings

1 Coat an unheated large skillet with nonstick cooking spray. Preheat skillet over medium heat. Add the potatoes, green onions, peppers, cumin, and garlic. Cook and stir about 3 minutes or until the vegetables are tender.

2 In a small bowl stir together egg product, milk, and cilantro; add to skillet. Cook, without stirring, until mixture begins to set on the bottom and around the edge. Using a spatula, lift and fold the partially cooked mixture so uncooked portion flows underneath. Continue cooking and folding until egg product is cooked through, but is still glossy and moist. Remove from heat.

3 To assemble pizza, place the bread shell on a large baking sheet or a 12-inch pizza pan. Sprinkle half of the cheese over the shell. Top with egg mixture, tomato, and the remaining cheese.

4 Bake in a 375° oven for 8 to 10 minutes or until cheese is melted. Cut into wedges to serve.

NUTRITION FACTS PER SERVING: 235 calories, 6 g total fat (1 g saturated fat), 8 mg cholesterol, 424 mg sodium, 33 g carbohydrate, 2 g fiber, 14 g protein.

Crustless Green Quiche

THIS HEALTHFUL RECIPE BRINGS YOU A DELICATE CHEESE AND
GREENS QUICHE WITHOUT A CALORIE- AND FAT-LADEN CRUST.

6 cups curly endive, escarole,
　　or frisée, washed and
　　stemmed
1 8-ounce carton refrigerated
　　or frozen egg product,
　　thawed
⅓ cup all-purpose flour
1 cup low-fat cottage cheese

2 green onions, chopped
　　(¼ cup)
⅛ teaspoon salt
⅛ teaspoon black pepper
⅛ teaspoon ground cumin
¼ cup finely shredded
　　Parmesan cheese

3 tablespoons canned diced
　　green chile peppers
Nonstick cooking spray
Fat-free dairy sour cream
　　(optional)
Sliced green onion
　　(optional)
Bottled salsa (optional)

EXCHANGES: ¹/₂ Starch, 1¹/₂ Lean Meat　**Prep:** 25 minutes　**Bake:** 30 minutes　**Makes:** 6 servings

1 Bring a large pot of lightly salted water to boiling. Add greens and cook about 1 minute or until limp. Drain. Cool and squeeze out excess moisture; chop. In blender container or food processor bowl combine egg product, flour, cottage cheese, chopped green onions, salt, black pepper, and cumin. Add greens. Cover and blend or process until combined. Stir in Parmesan cheese and chile peppers.

2 Coat a 9-inch pie plate with nonstick cooking spray. Pour batter into pie plate. Bake, uncovered, in a 350° oven for 30 to 35 minutes or until a knife inserted near the center comes out clean. Cut into wedges to serve. If desired, top with sour cream and sliced green onion. If desired, serve with salsa.

NUTRITION FACTS PER SERVING: 122 calories, 4 g total fat (1 g saturated fat), 7 mg cholesterol, 355 mg sodium, 10 g carbohydrate, 1 g fiber, 13 g protein.

Vegetable Quiches

QUICHE JUST GOT MORE HEALTHFUL WITH THIS EASY RECIPE THAT USES TORTILLAS FOR THE CRUST AND LOWER-FAT PRODUCTS IN PLACE OF TRADITIONAL INGREDIENTS.

Nonstick cooking spray

3 7- or 8-inch flour tortillas

½ cup shredded reduced-fat Swiss, cheddar, or mozzarella cheese (2 ounces)

1 cup broccoli flowerets

½ of a small red sweet pepper, cut into thin strips

2 green onions, sliced

1 8-ounce carton refrigerated or frozen egg product, thawed (about 1 cup)

¾ cup evaporated fat-free milk

¼ teaspoon dried thyme, crushed

⅛ teaspoon salt

⅛ teaspoon black pepper Thin strips red sweet pepper (optional)

EXCHANGES: ¹/₂ Starch, 1 Vegetable, 1 Lean Meat **Prep:** 25 minutes
Bake: 25 minutes **Stand::** 5 minutes **Makes:** 6 servings

---

1 Coat three 6- to 7-inch individual round baking dishes or pans* with nonstick cooking spray. Carefully press tortillas into dishes or pans. Sprinkle with cheese.

2 In a small covered saucepan cook the broccoli, the ¹/₂ cup sweet pepper strips, and the green onions in a small amount of boiling water about 3 minutes or until crisp-tender. Drain well. Sprinkle cooked vegetables over cheese in baking dishes.

3 In a medium bowl stir together egg product, evaporated milk, thyme, salt, and black pepper. Pour over vegetables in baking dishes. Place on baking sheet. Bake in a 375° oven for 25 to 30 minutes or until puffed and a knife inserted near center of each comes out clean. Let stand 5 minutes before serving. If desired, garnish with additional strips of sweet pepper.

NUTRITION FACTS PER SERVING: 133 calories, 4 g total fat (1 g saturated fat), 6 mg cholesterol, 333 mg sodium, 14 g carbohydrate, 1 g fiber, 10 g protein.

*Note: Or, coat six 6-ounce custard cups with nonstick cooking spray. Cut each tortilla into 6 wedges. To form crust, press 3 tortilla wedges into each custard cup with points toward center. Tortillas do not have to cover cups completely. Continue as above.

Spinach and Cheese Roll-Ups

NO TIME TO MAKE THE SAUCE FROM SCRATCH? USE BOTTLED SPAGHETTI SAUCE INSTEAD.

1 teaspoon olive oil or
cooking oil
⅓ cup chopped onion
1 clove garlic, minced
1 14½-ounce can tomatoes,
cut up
2 tablespoons tomato paste
1½ teaspoons snipped fresh
basil or ½ teaspoon dried
basil, crushed

¼ teaspoon sugar
Dash salt
Dash pepper
8 dried lasagna noodles
1 10-ounce package frozen
chopped spinach, thawed
¾ cup fat-free or low-fat
ricotta cheese
½ cup shredded part-skim
mozzarella cheese
(2 ounces)

2 tablespoons finely
shredded Parmesan
cheese
2 teaspoons snipped fresh
basil or ½ teaspoon dried
basil or Italian seasoning,
crushed
1 slightly beaten egg white
Fresh parsley sprigs
(optional)

EXCHANGES: 1½ Starch, 2 Vegetable, 1½ Lean Meat
Prep: 35 minutes **Bake:** 25 minutes **Makes:** 4 servings

1 For sauce, in a medium saucepan heat oil. Cook onion and garlic in hot oil until onion is tender, stirring occasionally. Carefully stir in undrained tomatoes, tomato paste, the 1½ teaspoons snipped basil, the sugar, salt, and pepper. Bring to boiling; reduce heat. Simmer, uncovered, about 5 minutes or until sauce is desired consistency, stirring occasionally.

2 Meanwhile, cook pasta according to package directions; drain. Rinse with cold water; drain well.

3 For filling, drain thawed spinach well, pressing out excess liquid. In a medium bowl stir together ricotta cheese, mozzarella cheese, Parmesan cheese, and the 2 teaspoons snipped basil. Add spinach and egg white, stirring to combine.

4 To assemble, evenly spread about ¼ cup filling on each noodle. Roll up from 1 end. Place 2 roll-ups, seam sides down, into each of 4 individual casseroles. Top with sauce.

5 Cover and bake casseroles in a 350° oven about 25 minutes or until heated through. If desired, garnish with parsley sprigs.

NUTRITION FACTS PER SERVING: 231 calories, 3 g total fat (0 g saturated fat), 10 mg cholesterol, 425 mg sodium, 39 g carbohydrate, 2 g fiber, 20 g protein.

Fettuccine with Eggplant Sauce

EGGPLANT SIMMERS WITH TOMATOES, SWEET PEPPERS,
AND BASIL TO CREATE A FULL-BODIED SAUCE FOR PASTA.

1 small eggplant (12 ounces)
2 tablespoons olive oil
½ cup chopped onion
1 clove garlic, minced
1 14 ½-ounce can Italian-style stewed tomatoes
1 15-ounce can low-sodium tomato sauce

1 medium green sweet pepper, cut into strips
2 teaspoons dried basil, crushed
1 teaspoon dried oregano, crushed
Salt
Black pepper

12 ounces dried fettuccine
Fresh basil sprigs (optional)

EXCHANGES: 3 Starch, 2 Vegetable, ¹/₂ Fat **Prep:** 20 minutes **Cook:** 40 minutes **Makes:** 6 servings

1 If desired, peel eggplant. Cut eggplant into ¹/₂-inch cubes.

2 In a large saucepan heat oil. Cook eggplant in hot oil about 7 minutes or until nearly tender. Add onion and garlic; cook and stir for 3 minutes more. Add undrained tomatoes, tomato sauce, sweet pepper, dried basil, and oregano. Bring to boiling; reduce heat. Cover and simmer for 30 minutes. Season to taste with salt and black pepper.

3 Meanwhile, cook the pasta according to package directions; drain and return to saucepan. Add sauce to pasta; toss to coat. If desired, garnish with basil sprigs.

NUTRITION FACTS PER SERVING: 319 calories, 6 g total fat (1 g saturated fat), 0 mg cholesterol, 255 mg sodium, 57 g carbohydrate, 4 g fiber, 9 g protein.

Vegetarian Delight

THIS BAYOU BLOCKBUSTER SIMMERS TOMATO, ZUCCHINI, AND CHICKPEAS INTO A CAJUN-STYLE STEW.

1 teaspoon olive oil	**1** 15-ounce can chickpeas (garbanzo beans), rinsed and drained	**½** teaspoon salt-free cajun seasoning
1 small onion, thinly sliced (⅓ cup)	**1** 14½-ounce can low-sodium diced tomatoes	Dash ground red pepper
2 medium zucchini, halved lengthwise and sliced	**1** 14½-ounce can low-sodium stewed tomatoes	**2** cups hot cooked couscous or brown rice
2 medium carrots, chopped		
2 cloves garlic, minced	**1** tablespoon sugar	
1 cup water		

EXCHANGES: 3 Starch, 5 Vegetable, 1 Very Lean Meat **Start to Finish:** 45 minutes **Makes:** 4 servings

1 In a large saucepan heat oil. Cook onion in hot oil for 5 minutes. Stir in zucchini, carrots, garlic, and ¼ cup of the water. Cook and stir for 3 minutes.

2 Stir in chickpeas, undrained diced tomatoes, undrained stewed tomatoes, sugar, cajun seasoning, ground red pepper, and the remaining water. Bring to boiling; reduce heat. Simmer, uncovered, about 20 minutes or until desired consistency.

3 Serve over couscous or brown rice.

NUTRITION FACTS PER SERVING: 314 calories, 3 g total fat (0 g saturated fat), 0 mg cholesterol, 415 mg sodium, 64 g carbohydrate, 11 g fiber, 11 g protein.

Barley-Stuffed Peppers

OLD-TIME STUFFED PEPPERS GO MEATLESS WITH THIS COLORFUL BARLEY STUFFING.

1 cup water
1 cup sliced fresh mushrooms
⅔ cup quick-cooking barley
½ of a vegetable bouillon cube
2 large red, yellow, and/or green sweet peppers (about 1 pound)
1 beaten egg

¾ cup shredded reduced-fat mozzarella cheese (3 ounces)
1 large tomato, peeled, seeded, and chopped (about ¾ cup)
½ cup shredded zucchini
⅓ cup soft bread crumbs
1 tablespoon snipped fresh basil or ½ teaspoon dried basil, crushed

1 teaspoon snipped fresh rosemary or ⅛ teaspoon dried rosemary, crushed
¼ teaspoon onion salt
Several dashes bottled hot pepper sauce
Fresh rosemary sprigs (optional)
Dried red chile peppers (optional)

EXCHANGES: 2 Starch, 1 Vegetable, 1 Lean Meat **Prep:** 20 minutes **Bake:** 22 minutes **Makes:** 4 servings

1 In a medium saucepan combine the water, mushrooms, uncooked barley, and bouillon. Bring to boiling; reduce heat. Cover and simmer for 12 to 15 minutes or until barley is tender. Drain well.

2 Cut sweet peppers in half lengthwise; remove seeds and membranes. If desired, precook pepper halves in boiling water for 3 minutes. Drain on paper towels.

3 In a medium bowl stir together the egg, ¹⁄₂ cup of the cheese, the tomato, zucchini, bread crumbs, basil, rosemary, onion salt, and bottled hot pepper sauce. Stir in cooked barley mixture. Place peppers, cut sides up, in a 2-quart rectangular baking dish. Spoon barley mixture into the pepper halves.

4 Cover and bake stuffed peppers in a 350° oven for 20 to 25 minutes or until filling is heated through. Sprinkle remaining cheese over the peppers. Return to oven; bake 2 minutes more. Carefully transfer peppers to a serving platter. If desired, garnish with rosemary sprigs and red chile peppers.

NUTRITION FACTS PER SERVING: 231 calories, 5 g total fat (3 g saturated fat), 65 mg cholesterol, 514 mg sodium, 33 g carbohydrate, 4 g fiber, 13 g protein.

Baked Brie Strata

THIS MAKE-AHEAD BRUNCH DISH SHOWCASES BUTTERY BRIE CHEESE LAYERED WITH ZUCCHINI AND CRUSTY SOURDOUGH BREAD.

2 small zucchini, cut crosswise into ¼-inch slices (about 2 cups)
Nonstick cooking spray
6 ½-inch-thick slices crusty sourdough bread
8 ounces Brie cheese, cut into ½-inch cubes

2 plum tomatoes, cut lengthwise into ¼-inch-thick slices
6 to 8 cherry tomatoes
1 cup refrigerated or frozen egg product, thawed
⅔ cup evaporated fat-free milk
⅓ cup finely chopped onion

3 tablespoons snipped fresh dill
¼ teaspoon salt
⅛ teaspoon pepper

EXCHANGES: 1 Starch, ¹/₂ Vegetable, 1 High-Fat Meat **Prep:** 25 minutes
Chill: 4 to 24 hours **Bake:** 55 minutes **Stand:** 10 minutes **Makes:** 8 servings

1 In a covered small saucepan cook zucchini in a small amount of boiling, lightly salted water for 2 to 3 minutes or just until tender. Drain zucchini. Set aside.

2 Meanwhile, coat a 2-quart rectangular baking dish with nonstick cooking spray. Arrange bread slices in the bottom of baking dish, cutting as necessary to fit. Sprinkle with half of the cheese. Arrange zucchini and tomatoes on top of bread. Sprinkle with the remaining cheese.

3 In a medium bowl combine egg product, evaporated milk, onion, dill, salt, and pepper. Pour evenly over vegetables and cheese. Press lightly with the back of a spoon to thoroughly moisten ingredients. Cover with plastic wrap and chill in the refrigerator for at least 4 hours or up to 24 hours.

4 Remove plastic wrap from strata; cover with foil. Bake in a 325° oven for 30 minutes. Uncover and bake for 25 to 30 minutes more or until a knife inserted near center comes out clean. Let stand for 10 minutes before serving.

NUTRITION FACTS PER SERVING: 189 calories, 9 g total fat (5 g saturated fat), 29 mg cholesterol, 441 mg sodium, 15 g carbohydrate, 1 g fiber, 13 g protein.

Tortellini Salad

A HOMEMADE BASIL DRESSING GIVES TORTELLINI ZESTY NEW FLAVOR.

2 tablespoons snipped fresh basil or 1 teaspoon dried basil, crushed

4 teaspoons powdered fruit pectin

1 tablespoon Dijon-style mustard

2 cloves garlic, minced

1 teaspoon sugar

¼ teaspoon pepper

⅓ cup water

2 tablespoon white wine vinegar or rice wine vinegar

1 9-ounce package refrigerated cheese tortellini

3 cups broccoli flowerets

1 cup sliced carrots

2 green onions, sliced (¼ cup)

1 large tomato, chopped

1 cup fresh pea pods, halved Lettuce leaves (optional)

EXCHANGES: 2¹/₂ Starch, 2 Vegetable, ¹/₂ Fat   **Prep:** 40 minutes   **Chill:** 2 to 24 hours   **Makes:** 4 servings

1 For dressing, in a small bowl stir together basil, pectin, mustard, garlic, sugar, and pepper. Stir in water and vinegar. Cover and chill in the refrigerator for 30 minutes.

2 Meanwhile, cook tortellini according to package directions, except omit any oil or salt. Add broccoli and carrots for the last 3 minutes of cooking. Drain. Rinse with cold running water; drain again.

3 In a large bowl combine the pasta mixture and green onions; drizzle with dressing. Toss to coat. Cover and chill in the refrigerator for at least 2 hours or up to 24 hours.

4 To serve, gently stir tomato and pea pods into salad. If desired, line 4 dinner plates with lettuce leaves. Top with pasta mixture.

NUTRITION FACTS PER SERVING: 269 calories, 5 g total fat (2 g saturated fat), 38 mg cholesterol, 328 mg sodium, 46 g carbohydrate, 6 g fiber, 12 g protein.

Chunky Minestrone

BIG SOUP IS THE TRANSLATION FOR THE ITALIAN WORD "MINESTRONE."
LOADED WITH BEANS AND VEGETABLES, THIS VERSION LIVES UP TO ITS NAME.

1 tablespoon olive oil
1½ cups chopped onion
1 medium carrot, halved lengthwise and thinly sliced (about ¾ cup)
2 cloves garlic, minced
3 cups vegetable broth or reduced-sodium chicken broth*
2 14½-ounce cans low-sodium tomatoes, cut up

¾ cup water
½ cup long grain rice
1 teaspoon dried Italian seasoning, crushed
4 cups shredded fresh spinach
1 15-ounce can navy beans or white kidney beans (cannellini beans), rinsed and drained

1 medium zucchini, quartered lengthwise and sliced (about 1½ cups)
¼ teaspoon pepper
Grated Parmesan cheese (optional)

EXCHANGES: 2 Starch, 3¹/₂ Vegetable, ¹/₂ Fat   **Prep:** 15 minutes   **Cook:** 25 minutes   **Makes:** 5 servings

1 In a Dutch oven heat oil over medium-high heat. Cook and stir onion, carrot, and garlic in hot oil about 3 minutes or until onion is tender. Stir in the broth, undrained tomatoes, water, uncooked rice, and Italian seasoning.

2 Bring to boiling; reduce heat. Cover and simmer about 20 minutes or until rice is tender. Stir in the spinach, beans, zucchini, and pepper. Cover and cook for 5 minutes more. If desired, sprinkle each serving with Parmesan cheese.

NUTRITION FACTS PER SERVING: 260 calories, 4 g total fat (1 g saturated fat), 0 mg cholesterol, 1,072 mg sodium, 50 g carbohydrate, 11 g fiber, 11 g protein.

*Note: If sodium is of concern, lower the sodium in this recipe by preparing it with the reduced-sodium chicken broth option. Or, prepare your own lightly salted vegetable broth.

Tortellini and Vegetable Soup

WILD RICE AND TORTELLINI PROVIDE A CONTRAST OF
TEXTURES AND FLAVORS IN THIS TANTALIZING VEGETABLE SOUP.

¼ cup wild rice
  Nonstick cooking spray
1 cup chopped onion
½ cup thinly sliced celery
1 clove garlic, minced
6½ cups water
1 vegetable bouillon cube*
1 teaspoon dried oregano,
  crushed

½ teaspoon dried marjoram,
  crushed
⅛ teaspoon pepper
1 bay leaf
1 9-ounce package
  refrigerated cheese
  tortellini
2 cups chopped broccoli
  flowerets

2 tablespoons snipped dried
  tomato (not oil-packed)

EXCHANGES: 2 Starch, 2 Vegetable, 1 Medium-Fat Meat **Start to Finish:** 1 hour **Makes:** 4 servings

1 Rinse wild rice in a strainer under cold running water about 1 minute. Drain; set aside.

2 Coat an unheated large saucepan with nonstick cooking spray. Preheat over medium-high heat. Add onion, celery, and garlic. Cover and cook for 3 to 4 minutes or until vegetables are crisp-tender, stirring once or twice. Carefully stir in wild rice, the water, bouillon, oregano, marjoram, pepper, and bay leaf. Bring to boiling; reduce heat. Cover and simmer about 35 minutes or until rice is nearly tender. Discard bay leaf.

3 Add tortellini, broccoli, and dried tomato. Return to boiling; reduce heat. Cook, uncovered, for 5 to 6 minutes more or until tortellini and broccoli are just tender. To serve, ladle soup into bowls.

NUTRITION FACTS PER SERVING: 277 calories, 5 g total fat (2 g saturated fat), 30 mg cholesterol, 746 mg sodium, 46 g carbohydrate, 4 g fiber, 15 g protein.

*Note: If sodium is of concern, lower the sodium in this recipe by preparing it with 2 teaspoons instant low-sodium chicken bouillon granules in place of the vegetable bouillon cube. Or, prepare your own lightly salted vegetable broth or stock and substitute it for the water and the vegetable bouillon cube.

Sides & Desserts

ROUND OUT HEALTHFUL MEALS WITH THESE CAPTIVATING VEGETABLES, SALADS, AND BREADS, PLUS TARTS, CAKES, AND OTHER DESSERTS.

Chocolate Ice Cream Roll **page 268**

Lemony Mixed Vegetables

ORDINARY GREEN BEANS TAKE ON NEW CHARACTER WHEN
THEY'RE SERVED IN THIS BOLD HERB AND LEMON SAUCE.

1 cup reduced-sodium
   chicken broth
¼ teaspoon ground coriander
⅛ teaspoon salt
⅛ teaspoon black pepper
8 ounces fresh green beans,
   cut into 2-inch pieces
   (about 2 cups)

2 cups thinly bias-sliced carrots
1 cup cauliflower flowerets
½ of a medium red sweet
   pepper, cut into 1-inch
   pieces
1 tablespoon snipped fresh
   oregano or 1 teaspoon
   dried oregano, crushed

1 tablespoon cold water
1½ teaspoons cornstarch
½ teaspoon finely shredded
   lemon peel
4 teaspoons lemon juice

EXCHANGES: 2 Vegetable **Start to Finish:** 30 minutes **Makes:** 6 servings

1 In a large saucepan combine broth, coriander, salt, and black pepper. Bring to boiling; add green beans. Return to boiling; reduce heat. Cover and simmer for 10 minutes. Add carrots, cauliflower, and sweet pepper. Return to boiling; reduce heat. Cover and simmer for 4 to 5 minutes more or until vegetables are crisp-tender.

2 Using a slotted spoon, transfer vegetables to a serving bowl, reserving broth mixture in saucepan. Cover vegetables; keep warm.

3 In a small bowl stir together oregano, water, cornstarch, and lemon peel; stir into broth mixture in saucepan. Cook and stir over medium heat until slightly thickened and bubbly. Cook and stir for 2 minutes more. Stir in lemon juice. Pour thickened broth mixture over vegetables. Toss lightly to coat.

NUTRITION FACTS PER SERVING: 49 calories, 0 g total fat (0 g saturated fat), 0 mg cholesterol, 184 mg sodium, 11 g carbohydrate, 3 g fiber, 2 g protein.

Vegetable Primavera

SQUASH, CARROTS, RED PEPPER, AND BROCCOLI
TEAM UP TO CREATE A CULINARY KALEIDOSCOPE.

3 tablespoons reduced-
sodium chicken broth
1 tablespoon Dijon-style
mustard
1 tablespoon olive oil
2 teaspoons white wine
vinegar

Nonstick cooking spray
1½ cups sliced yellow summer
squash
1 cup packaged, peeled baby
carrots
1 cup chopped red sweet
pepper

3 cups broccoli flowerets
2 tablespoons snipped fresh
parsley

EXCHANGES: 1 Vegetable, ½ Fat **Start to Finish:** 20 minutes **Makes:** 6 servings

1 In a small bowl combine 1 tablespoon of the broth, the mustard, oil, and vinegar. Set aside.

2 Coat an unheated large nonstick skillet with nonstick cooking spray. Preheat the skillet over medium heat. Cook and stir squash, carrots, and sweet pepper in hot skillet about 5 minutes or until nearly tender. Add broccoli and remaining broth to skillet. Cover and cook about 3 minutes or until broccoli is crisp-tender.

3 Stir in the mustard mixture; heat through. To serve, sprinkle with parsley.

NUTRITION FACTS PER SERVING: 56 calories, 3 g total fat (0 g saturated fat), 0 mg cholesterol, 114 mg sodium, 7 g carbohydrate, 3 g fiber, 2 g protein.

Orange-Sauced Broccoli and Peppers

PREPARE THIS GARDEN-FRESH COMBO NEXT TIME YOU GRILL PORK OR CHICKEN. FOR EXTRA COLOR, USE HALF OF A RED AND HALF OF A YELLOW SWEET PEPPER.

3½ cups broccoli flowerets	**2** tablespoons finely chopped onion
1 medium red or yellow sweet pepper, cut into bite-size strips	**1** clove garlic, minced
	1½ teaspoons cornstarch
1 tablespoon butter or margarine	**⅔** cup orange juice
	2 teaspoons Dijon-style mustard

EXCHANGES: 1 Vegetable, ¹/₂ Fat **Start to Finish:** 20 minutes **Makes:** 6 servings

1 In a medium saucepan cook broccoli and sweet pepper in a small amount of boiling lightly salted water about 8 minutes or until broccoli is crisp-tender; drain. Cover and keep warm.

2 Meanwhile, for sauce, in a small saucepan melt butter or margarine over medium heat. Cook onion and garlic in butter or margarine until onion is tender. Stir in cornstarch. Add orange juice and mustard. Cook and stir until mixture is thickened and bubbly. Cook and stir for 2 minutes more.

3 To serve, pour sauce over broccoli mixture. Toss gently to coat.

NUTRITION FACTS PER SERVING: 58 calories, 2 g total fat (1 g saturated fat), 5 mg cholesterol, 82 mg sodium, 8 g carbohydrate, 3 g fiber, 2 g protein.

Vegetable Strudel

THIS FLAKY PHYLLO STRUDEL STUFFED WITH VEGETABLES AND CHEESE MAKES A GREAT SERVE-ALONG FOR SOUP OR SALAD.

5 cups fresh spinach leaves	**4** green onions, sliced (½ cup)	⅛ teaspoon salt
4 cups water	¼ cup oil-packed dried tomatoes, drained and chopped	⅛ teaspoon black pepper
2 medium red sweet peppers, cut into 1-inch strips		Dash ground red pepper
1 medium yellow summer squash, cut into 1-inch strips	**3** tablespoons grated Parmesan cheese	Butter-flavored nonstick cooking spray
2 carrots, shredded	**1** tablespoon snipped fresh oregano or ½ teaspoon dried oregano, crushed	**6** sheets frozen phyllo dough, thawed
½ cup sliced fresh mushrooms		**2** tablespoons fine dry bread crumbs

EXCHANGES: ½ Starch, 1½ Vegetable **Prep:** 40 minutes
Bake: 25 minutes **Stand:** 10 minutes **Makes:** 8 servings

1 For filling, place the spinach in large colander. Set aside. In a large saucepan bring the water to boiling. Cook sweet peppers, summer squash, carrots, mushrooms, and green onions in boiling water for 2 to 3 minutes or until vegetables are crisp-tender. Pour over spinach to drain; rinse immediately with cold water. Drain well, pressing out excess moisture. Transfer vegetables to a large bowl. Stir in the dried tomatoes, 2 tablespoons of the Parmesan cheese, the oregano, salt, black pepper, and ground red pepper. Set aside.

2 Coat a large baking sheet with nonstick cooking spray. Set aside. Place 1 sheet of the phyllo on a dry kitchen towel. (Keep remaining sheets covered with plastic wrap to prevent drying out.) Coat with nonstick cooking spray. Place another sheet on top; coat with nonstick cooking spray. Sprinkle with half of the bread crumbs. Place 2 more sheets of the phyllo on top, coating each with nonstick cooking spray. Sprinkle with remaining bread crumbs. Add remaining 2 sheets of phyllo, coating each with nonstick cooking spray.

3 Spoon filling along 1 long side of phyllo stack about 1½ inches from edges. Fold the short sides over the filling. Starting from the long side with filling, roll up into a spiral.

4 Place strudel, seam side down, on the prepared baking sheet. Coat top with nonstick cooking spray. Using a sharp knife, score into 8 slices, cutting through the top layer only. Sprinkle with remaining Parmesan cheese.

5 Bake in a 375° oven for 25 to 30 minutes or until the strudel is golden. Let stand for 10 minutes before serving. To serve, cut along scored lines into slices.

NUTRITION FACTS PER SERVING: 88 calories, 2 g total fat (1 g saturated fat), 1 mg cholesterol, 214 mg sodium, 14 g carbohydrate, 4 g fiber, 4 g protein.

Chilled Asparagus Salad

REMEMBER THIS CHILLED COMBINATION WHEN YOU NEED A SALAD FOR A COOKOUT.

½ cup fat-free mayonnaise dressing or salad dressing
¼ cup plain fat-free yogurt
½ teaspoon finely shredded orange peel
⅓ cup orange juice

⅛ teaspoon lemon-pepper seasoning
1½ pounds fresh asparagus spears or two 10-ounce packages frozen asparagus spears

Orange peel strips (optional)

EXCHANGES: 2 Vegetable **Prep:** 20 minutes **Chill:** 30 minutes **Makes:** 6 servings

1 For dressing, in a small bowl stir together mayonnaise dressing or salad dressing, yogurt, shredded orange peel, orange juice, and lemon-pepper seasoning. Cover and chill in the refrigerator until serving time.

2 If using fresh asparagus, snap off and discard woody bases. If desired, scrape off scales. Cook in a covered saucepan in a small amount of boiling water about 8 minutes or until crisp-tender. If using frozen asparagus, cook according to package directions.

3 Drain asparagus. Immediately plunge cooked asparagus into ice water. When chilled, drain. Cover and chill in the refrigerator at least 30 minutes or until serving time.

4 Just before serving, arrange chilled asparagus spears on serving plates. Drizzle dressing over asparagus. If desired, garnish with orange peel strips.

NUTRITION FACTS PER SERVING: 47 calories, 0 g total fat (0 g saturated fat), 0 mg cholesterol, 287 mg sodium, 10 g carbohydrate, 2 g fiber, 3 g protein.

Tropical Coffee Cake

THE YOGURT AND COOKING OIL IN THIS EXCEPTIONAL CAKE HELP KEEP IT MOIST.

1¼ cups all-purpose flour	¼ teaspoon salt	1 medium mango, peeled, seeded, and finely chopped (about 1 cup)
¼ cup sugar plus 4 packets heat-stable sugar substitute, or ½ cup sugar	¼ teaspoon ground nutmeg	1 tablespoon all-purpose flour
	1 beaten egg	2 tablespoons flaked coconut
	⅔ cup plain fat-free yogurt	
½ teaspoon baking powder	2 tablespoons cooking oil	
½ teaspoon baking soda	½ teaspoon vanilla	

EXCHANGES: 1½ Starch, ½ Fruit, ½ Fat **Prep:** 25 minutes **Bake:** 35 minutes **Makes:** 8 servings

1 Lightly grease and flour a 9×1½-inch round baking pan. Set aside. In a large bowl stir together the 1¼ cups flour, the sugar plus sugar substitute or the sugar, baking powder, baking soda, salt, and nutmeg. Make a well in the center of the flour mixture. Set aside.

2 In a small bowl stir together the egg, yogurt, oil, and vanilla. Add the egg mixture all at once to flour mixture. Stir just until moistened (batter should be slightly lumpy). Toss chopped mango with the 1 tablespoon flour; gently fold into batter. Spread batter into prepared pan.

3 Sprinkle coconut over batter in pan. Bake in a 350° oven for 35 minutes. Serve warm.

NUTRITION FACTS PER SERVING: 169 calories, 5 g total fat (1 g saturated fat), 27 mg cholesterol, 194 mg sodium, 28 g carbohydrate, 1 g fiber, 4 g protein.

Raspberry and Cheese Coffee Cake

WHETHER YOU SERVE IT FOR A SNACK, BREAKFAST, OR DESSERT,
THIS CALORIE-CONSCIOUS COFFEE CAKE IS SURE TO BE A HIT.

Nonstick cooking spray
1¼ cups all-purpose flour
1¼ teaspoons baking powder
1 teaspoon finely shredded
    lemon peel or orange peel
¼ teaspoon baking soda
¼ teaspoon salt
¾ cup granulated sugar
3 tablespoons butter,
    softened

¼ cup refrigerated or frozen
    egg product, thawed
1 teaspoon vanilla
½ cup buttermilk
2 ounces reduced-fat cream
    cheese (Neufchâtel)
¼ cup granulated sugar
2 tablespoons refrigerated or
    frozen egg product,
    thawed

1 cup raspberries or thinly
    sliced apricots or
    nectarines*
Raspberries or thinly sliced
    apricots or nectarines
    (optional)`
Sifted powdered sugar
Fresh mint sprigs (optional)

EXCHANGES: 2 Starch, 1 Fat **Prep:** 20 minutes **Bake:** 30 minutes **Makes:** 10 servings

1 Coat a 9×1½-inch round baking pan with nonstick cooking spray. Set aside. In a medium bowl stir together the flour, baking powder, lemon peel or orange peel, baking soda, and salt. Set aside.

2 In medium bowl beat the ¾ cup granulated sugar and the butter with an electric mixer on medium to high speed until combined. Add the ¼ cup egg product and the vanilla. Beat on low to medium speed for 1 minute. Add the flour mixture and buttermilk alternately to the egg mixture, beating just until combined after each addition. Pour into prepared pan.

3 In a small bowl beat the cream cheese and the ¼ cup granulated sugar on medium to high speed until combined. Add the 2 tablespoons egg product. Beat until combined. Arrange the 1 cup fruit over the batter in the pan. Pour the cream cheese mixture over all. Bake in a 375° oven for 30 to 35 minutes or until a wooden toothpick inserted near center comes out clean. Cool slightly on wire rack. Serve warm. If desired, top with additional fruit. Dust with powdered sugar. If desired, garnish with mint sprigs.

NUTRITION FACTS PER SERVING: 195 calories, 5 g total fat (3 g saturated fat), 9 mg cholesterol, 223 mg sodium, 33 g carbohydrate, 1 g fiber, 4 g protein.

*Note: If you like, substitute well-drained, thinly sliced canned apricots or peach slices for the fresh fruit.

Easy Herb Focaccia **top**;
Parmesan and Pine Nut
Focaccia **bottom**

Easy Herb Focaccia

THIS EASY-FIXIN' FOCACCIA (FOH-KAH-CHEE-AH) IS
DELICIOUS WITH EVERYTHING FROM PASTA TO SOUP TO SALADS.

Nonstick cooking spray
1 16-ounce package hot
roll mix
1 egg
2 tablespoons olive oil
2 teaspoons olive oil

⅔ cup finely chopped onion
1 teaspoon dried rosemary,
crushed

EXCHANGES: 1 Starch **Prep:** 20 minutes **Rise:** 30 minutes **Bake:** 15 minutes **Makes:** 24 servings

1 Coat a 15×10×1-inch baking pan or a 12- to 14-inch pizza pan with nonstick cooking spray. Set aside.

2 Prepare the hot roll mix according to package directions for the basic dough, using the 1 egg and substituting the 2 tablespoons oil for the margarine. Knead dough; allow to rest as directed. If using the large baking pan, roll dough into a 15×10-inch rectangle and carefully transfer to prepared pan. If using the pizza pan, roll dough into a 12-inch circle and carefully transfer to prepared pan.

3 In a small skillet heat the 2 teaspoons oil. Cook onion and rosemary in the hot oil until tender. With fingertips, press indentations every inch or so in dough. Top dough evenly with onion mixture. Cover and let rise in a warm place until nearly double (about 30 minutes).

4 Bake in a 375° oven for 15 to 20 minutes or until golden. Cool in pan for 10 minutes on a wire rack. Remove focaccia from pan; cool completely on wire rack.

NUTRITION FACTS PER SERVING: 95 calories, 3 g total fat (0 g saturated fat), 9 mg cholesterol, 122 mg sodium, 15 g carbohydrate, 0 g fiber, 4 g protein.

Parmesan and Pine Nut Focaccia: Prepare Easy Herb Focaccia as above, except omit the 2 teaspoons olive oil, the onion, and rosemary. Make the indentations, then brush the dough with a mixture of 1 egg white and 2 tablespoons water. Sprinkle with ¼ cup pine nuts, pressing lightly into dough. Sprinkle with 2 tablespoons freshly grated Parmesan cheese. Bake as directed.

Nutmeg-Apricot Rolls

TAKE YOUR CHOICE—BAKE THESE FRUITY SPIRALS RIGHT AWAY
OR HOLD THEM IN THE REFRIGERATOR TO BAKE THE NEXT DAY.

---

4 to 4⅓ cups all-purpose flour
2 packages active dry yeast
1 cup fat-free milk
⅓ cup granulated sugar
3 tablespoons butter
½ teaspoon salt
2 eggs

Nonstick cooking spray
½ cup applesauce
3 tablespoons granulated
  sugar
½ teaspoon ground nutmeg
⅔ cup snipped dried apricots,
  raisins, or dried cherries

1 cup sifted powdered sugar
1 teaspoon vanilla
2 to 3 teaspoons apricot
  nectar or orange juice

EXCHANGES: 1 Starch, 1 Fruit **Prep:** 45 minutes **Rise:** 1½ hours **Bake:** 20 minutes **Makes:** 24 rolls

---

1 In a large bowl stir together 1½ cups of the flour and the yeast. Set aside. In a medium saucepan heat and stir the milk, the ⅓ cup granulated sugar, the butter, and salt just until warm (120° to 130°) and butter almost melts. Add milk mixture and eggs to the flour mixture. Beat with an electric mixer on low to medium speed for 30 seconds, scraping the side of the bowl constantly. Beat on high speed for 3 minutes. Using a wooden spoon, stir in as much of the remaining flour as you can.

2 Turn the dough out onto a lightly floured surface. Knead in enough of the remaining flour to make a moderately soft dough that is smooth and elastic (3 to 5 minutes total). Shape the dough into a ball. Place dough in a lightly greased bowl, turning once to grease surface of the dough. Cover and let rise in a warm place until double in size (about 1 hour).

3 Punch dough down. Turn dough out onto a lightly floured surface. Divide dough in half. Cover; let rest for 10 minutes. Meanwhile, coat two 9×1½-inch round baking pans with nonstick cooking spray.

4 Roll each half of the dough into a 12×8-inch rectangle. Spread the applesauce over the dough. In a small bowl stir together the 3 tablespoons granulated sugar and the nutmeg. Sprinkle the sugar mixture over the applesauce. Sprinkle the apricots, raisins, or cherries over the sugar mixture. Roll up each rectangle into a spiral, starting from 1 of the long sides. Pinch seams to seal. Cut each spiral into 12 pieces. Place pieces, cut sides down, in the prepared pans. Cover; let rise until nearly double (about 30 minutes). (Or, cover with oiled waxed paper, then with plastic wrap and chill in the refrigerator for at least 2 hours or up to 24 hours.)

5 If chilled, let stand, covered, for 20 minutes at room temperature. Puncture any surface bubbles with a greased wooden toothpick. Bake in a 375° oven for 20 to 25 minutes or until golden brown. Cool in pans on wire racks for 5 minutes. Remove from pans. Cool completely on a wire rack.

6 Meanwhile, in a small bowl stir together powdered sugar and vanilla. Stir in enough of the apricot nectar or orange juice to make of drizzling consistency. Drizzle over rolls.

NUTRITION FACTS PER ROLL: 141 calories, 2 g total fat (1 g saturated fat), 22 mg cholesterol, 73 mg sodium, 27 g carbohydrate, 1 g fiber, 3 g protein.

Parmesan Corn Bread Puffs

FOR BEST FLAVOR AND TEXTURE, BE SURE TO ENJOY THESE PUFFS WARM.

Nonstick cooking spray
½ cup all-purpose flour
⅓ cup yellow cornmeal
4 teaspoons sugar
1 teaspoon baking powder
Dash salt
1 slightly beaten egg white
⅓ cup fat-free milk

2 tablespoons cooking oil
2 tablespoons grated
Parmesan cheese

EXCHANGES: ½ Starch, ½ Fat **Prep:** 15 minutes **Bake:** 10 minutes **Cool:** 5 minutes **Makes:** 12 puffs

---

1 Coat twelve 1¾-inch muffin cups with nonstick cooking spray. Set aside.

2 In a large bowl stir together flour, cornmeal, sugar, baking powder, and salt. Stir together egg white, milk, and oil. Add egg white mixture to the flour mixture, stirring just until smooth. Spoon into prepared muffin cups, filling each about three-fourths full.

3 Bake in a 425° oven for 10 to 12 minutes or until golden brown. Remove from pan. Cool on a wire rack for 5 minutes. Place cheese in a plastic bag. Add warm puffs a few at a time; toss to coat with cheese. Serve warm.

NUTRITION FACTS PER PUFF: 69 calories, 3 g total fat (1 g saturated fat), 1 mg cholesterol, 40 mg sodium, 9 g carbohydrate, 0 g fiber, 2 g protein.

Pumpkin Muffins

BUCKWHEAT FLOUR IS THE SECRET INGREDIENT IN THESE MOIST, RICH MUFFINS.

Nonstick cooking spray
1⅓ cups all-purpose flour
¾ cup buckwheat flour
¼ cup sugar plus 2 packages heat-stable sugar substitute or ⅓ cup sugar
1½ teaspoons baking powder

1 teaspoon ground cinnamon
½ teaspoon baking soda
½ teaspoon salt
2 slightly beaten eggs
1 cup canned pumpkin
½ cup fat-free milk
2 tablespoons cooking oil

½ teaspoon finely shredded orange peel
¼ cup orange juice

EXCHANGES: 1½ Starch, ½ Fat **Prep:** 20 minutes **Bake:** 15 minutes **Makes:** 12 muffins

1 Coat twelve 2½-inch muffin cups with nonstick cooking spray. Set aside. In a medium bowl combine the all-purpose flour, buckwheat flour, sugar plus sugar substitute or the sugar, baking powder, cinnamon, baking soda, and salt. Make a well in the center of flour mixture. Set aside.

2 In another bowl combine the eggs, pumpkin, milk, oil, orange peel, and orange juice. Add the egg mixture all at once to the flour mixture. Stir just until moistened (batter should be lumpy).

3 Spoon batter evenly into the prepared muffin cups. Bake in a 400° oven for 15 to 20 minutes or until the muffins are light brown. Cool in muffin cups on wire rack for 5 minutes. Remove from muffin cups; serve warm.

NUTRITION FACTS PER MUFFIN: 134 calories, 4 g total fat (1 g saturated fat), 36 mg cholesterol, 204 mg sodium, 22 g carbohydrate, 2 g fiber, 4 g protein.

Summer Fruit Tart

ANY TYPE OF SUMMER FRUIT YOU LIKE WORKS WELL FOR THIS CREAMY TART.

1¼ cups all-purpose flour	¼ cup refrigerated or frozen egg product, thawed	½ cup fresh blueberries, raspberries, and/or blackberries
¼ teaspoon salt	½ teaspoon vanilla	
¼ cup shortening	2 medium nectarines or peeled peaches, thinly sliced	2 tablespoons honey
4 to 5 tablespoons cold water		1 tablespoon rum or orange juice
¼ cup sugar	2 plums, thinly sliced	
2 tablespoons cornstarch	2 kiwi fruit, peeled and sliced	
1 12-ounce can evaporated fat-free milk		

EXCHANGES: 1 Starch, 1 Fruit, 1 Fat **Prep:** 35 minutes
Bake: 10 minutes **Chill:** 1 hour +1 hour **Makes:** 10 servings

1 For pastry, in a medium bowl stir together flour and salt. Cut in shortening until mixture resembles fine crumbs. Sprinkle 1 tablespoon of the water over part of mixture; gently toss with fork. Repeat until all is moistened. Form into ball. On a lightly floured surface, flatten dough. Roll out dough to form a circle 13 inches in diameter. Ease pastry into an 11-inch tart pan with removable bottom, being careful not to stretch pastry. Trim even with edge of pan. Prick pastry well with a fork. Bake in a 450° oven for 10 to 12 minutes or until golden brown. Cool completely.

2 For filling, in a heavy, medium saucepan combine sugar and cornstarch; stir in the evaporated milk and egg product. Cook and stir over medium heat until mixture is thickened and bubbly. Cook and stir for 2 minutes more. Remove from heat. Stir in vanilla. Cover surface with plastic wrap and chill in the refrigerator for 1 to 2 hours or until thoroughly chilled.

3 Spread chilled filling in tart shell. Arrange nectarines, plums, and kiwi fruit over filling. Sprinkle with berries. In a small bowl combine honey and rum or orange juice; brush on fruit. Cover and chill in the refrigerator for up to 1 hour. To serve, remove side of pan.

NUTRITION FACTS PER SERVING: 187 calories, 6 g total fat (1 g saturated fat), 1 mg cholesterol, 84 mg sodium, 31 g carbohydrate, 2 g fiber, 4 g protein.

Country Apricot Tart

NO NEED TO FUSS WITH CRIMPING THE EDGE OF THIS TART; JUST FOLD THE CORNMEAL CRUST OVER THE FRUIT FILLING.

1 recipe Cornmeal Crust
3 tablespoons sugar plus
  3 packets heat-stable
  sugar substitute or ⅓ cup
  sugar
3 tablespoons all-purpose flour
¼ teaspoon ground nutmeg or
  ground cinnamon

3 cups sliced, pitted fresh
  apricots or 3 cups frozen,
  unsweetened peach slices,
  thawed (do not drain)
1 tablespoon lemon juice
2 teaspoons fat-free milk

EXCHANGES: 1 Starch, 1 Fruit, 1 Fat **Prep:** 30 minutes **Bake:** 40 minutes **Cool:** 30 minutes **Makes:** 8 servings

1 Grease and lightly flour a large baking sheet. Prepare Cornmeal Crust. On the baking sheet, flatten dough. Roll into a circle 12 inches in diameter. Set aside.

2 For filling, in a bowl stir together sugar plus sugar substitute or sugar, flour, and nutmeg or cinnamon. Stir in apricots or peaches and lemon juice. Mound the filling in center of crust, leaving a 2-inch border. Fold border up over filling. Brush top and side of crust with the milk.

3 Bake in a 375° oven about 40 minutes or until crust in golden and filling is bubbly. To prevent over-browning, cover the edge of crust with foil for the last 10 to 15 minutes of baking. Cool tart for 30 minutes on the baking sheet on a wire rack. Serve warm.

Cornmeal Crust: In a medium bowl stir together ¾ cup flour, ⅓ cup cornmeal, 2 tablespoons sugar, 1 teaspoon baking powder, and ⅛ teaspoon salt. Cut in 3 tablespoons butter until the size of small peas. Sprinkle 1 tablespoon cold fat-free milk over mixture; gently toss with a fork. Add an additional 3 to 4 tablespoons fat-free milk, 1 tablespoon at a time, until the dough is moistened (dough will be crumbly). Turn out onto a lightly floured surface and knead 7 or 8 times or just until dough clings together. Form into a ball.

NUTRITION FACTS PER SERVING: 176 calories, 5 g total fat (3 g saturated fat), 12 mg cholesterol, 128 mg sodium, 32 g carbohydrate, 2 g fiber, 3 g protein.

Strawberry Cream Pie

DELICATE LADYFINGERS CRADLE A BERRY MOUSSE IN THIS SUMPTUOUS DESSERT.

2½ cups fresh strawberries	**3** slightly beaten egg whites	**½** of an 8-ounce container
¼ cup sugar	**1** tablespoon tequila or	frozen light whipped
1 envelope unflavored gelatin	orange juice	dessert topping, thawed
2 tablespoons frozen limeade	**1** 3-ounce package	Sliced fresh strawberries
concentrate or frozen	ladyfingers, split	(optional)
lemonade concentrate,	**2** tablespoons orange juice	Fresh mint (optional)
thawed		

EXCHANGES: 1 Starch, ¹/₂ Fruit, ¹/₂ Fat **Prep:** 30 minutes **Chill:** 2 hours + 2 hours **Makes:** 8 servings

1 Place the 2¹/₂ cups strawberries in a blender container or food processor bowl. Cover and blend or process until nearly smooth. Measure strawberries (you should have about 1¹/₂ cups).

2 In a medium saucepan stir together the sugar and gelatin. Stir in the blended strawberries and limeade concentrate or lemonade concentrate. Cook and stir over medium heat until the mixture bubbles and the gelatin is dissolved. Gradually stir about half of the gelatin mixture into the egg whites. Return mixture to saucepan. Cook, stirring constantly, over low heat about 3 minutes or until mixture is slightly thickened. Do not boil. Pour into a medium bowl; stir in tequila or orange juice. Chill in the refrigerator about 2 hours or until mixture mounds when spooned, stirring occasionally.

3 Meanwhile, cut half of the split ladyfingers in half crosswise; stand on end around the outside edge of a 9-inch tart pan with a removable bottom or a 9-inch springform pan. Arrange remaining split ladyfingers in the bottom of the pan. Drizzle the 2 tablespoons orange juice over the ladyfingers.

4 Fold whipped topping into strawberry mixture. Spoon into prepared pan. Cover and chill in the refrigerator about 2 hours or until set. If desired, garnish with the sliced strawberries and mint.

NUTRITION FACTS PER SERVING: 130 calories, 3 g total fat (2 g saturated fat), 39 mg cholesterol, 48 mg sodium, 22 g carbohydrate, 1 g fiber, 4 g protein.

Sweet-Topped Raspberries

YOGURT MIXED WITH LIGHT WHIPPED TOPPING IS A LUSCIOUS LOW-FAT
SUBSTITUTE FOR WHIPPED CREAM ON THIS DESSERT—OR ANY OTHER.

½ teaspoon finely shredded
   orange peel
2 tablespoons orange juice
2 cups fresh raspberries,
   blueberries, or sliced
   strawberries

½ cup thawed frozen light or
   fat-free whipped dessert
   topping
¼ cup vanilla low-fat yogurt
   Finely shredded orange
   peel (optional)

EXCHANGES: 1 Fruit **Start to Finish:** 10 minutes **Makes:** 4 servings

1 In a medium bowl stir together the ½ teaspoon orange peel and the orange juice. Add the berries; toss to coat.

2 For topping, in a small bowl stir together the dessert topping and yogurt.

3 Divide berry mixture among 4 dessert dishes. Spoon some of the topping over each serving. If desired, sprinkle with additional finely shredded orange peel. Serve immediately.

NUTRITION FACTS PER SERVING: 57 calories, 1 g total fat (1 g saturated fat), 1 mg cholesterol, 12 mg sodium, 11 g carbohydrate, 3 g fiber, 1 g protein.

Lemon Cream

ELEGANT, YET EASY TO MAKE, THIS LEMON DESSERT GETS ITS CITRUSY PIZZAZZ FROM BOTH LEMON PEEL AND LEMON JUICE.

¼ cup sugar
1 envelope unflavored gelatin
1½ cups water
2 slightly beaten eggs
1 tablespoon finely shredded
    lemon peel
⅓ cup lemon juice

½ of an 8-ounce container
    frozen light whipped
    dessert topping, thawed
Lemon peel strips (optional)

EXCHANGES: 1 Starch, ½ Fat **Prep:** 55 minutes **Chill:** 2 hours **Makes:** 6 servings

1 In a medium saucepan combine the sugar and gelatin; stir in water. Cook and stir over medium heat until mixture bubbles and gelatin is dissolved. Gradually stir about half of the gelatin mixture into the slightly beaten eggs. Return the mixture to the saucepan. Cook, stirring constantly, over low heat for 2 to 3 minutes or until slightly thickened.

2 Transfer to a medium bowl. Stir in the shredded lemon peel and lemon juice. Chill in an ice water bath about 20 minutes or just until the mixture thickens slightly, stirring occasionally.

3 Fold whipped topping into the lemon mixture. Chill again in an ice water bath about 15 minutes or just until mixture mounds, stirring occasionally.

4 Spoon into individual dessert dishes or soufflé dishes. Cover and chill in the refrigerator for at least 2 hours or until set. If desired, garnish with lemon peel strips.

NUTRITION FACTS PER SERVING: 107 calories, 4 g total fat (3 g saturated fat), 71 mg cholesterol, 37 mg sodium, 15 g carbohydrate, 0 g fiber, 3 g protein.

Chocolate Ice Cream Roll

WHAT COULD BE MORE TEMPTING THAN CHOCOLATE CAKE
AND ICE CREAM ROLLED INTO ONE? (PICTURED ON PAGE 231.)

⅓ cup all-purpose flour	⅓ cup granulated sugar	1 recipe Raspberry Sauce
¼ cup unsweetened	4 egg whites	(optional)
cocoa powder	½ cup granulated sugar	Fresh raspberries (optional)
1 teaspoon baking powder	Sifted powdered sugar	Fresh mint sprigs (optional)
¼ teaspoon salt	1 quart fat-free vanilla	
4 egg yolks	ice cream, softened	
½ teaspoon vanilla	¼ cup broken pecans, toasted	

EXCHANGES: 2 Starch, 1 Fat **Prep:** 30 minutes
Bake: 12 minutes **Cool:** 1 hour **Freeze:** 4 hours **Makes:** 12 servings

1 Grease and flour a 15×10×1-inch baking pan. In a large bowl stir together flour, cocoa powder, baking powder, and salt. Set aside. In a small bowl beat egg yolks and vanilla with an electric mixer on high speed about 5 minutes or until lemon-colored. Gradually add the ⅓ cup granulated sugar, beating on medium speed about 5 minutes or until sugar is almost dissolved. Wash and dry beaters.

2 In a large bowl beat egg whites on high speed until soft peaks form. Add the ½ cup granulated sugar, beating until stiff peaks form (tips stand straight). Fold yolk mixture into egg white mixture. Sprinkle flour mixture over egg mixture; fold in gently. Spread batter into prepared pan. Bake in a 375° oven for 12 to 15 minutes or until top springs back when lightly touched.

3 Meanwhile, sprinkle a clean dish towel with powdered sugar. Loosen edges of hot cake from pan; turn out onto prepared towel. Starting with a narrow end, roll up cake and towel together. Cool on wire rack for 1 hour.

4 Unroll cake. Spread ice cream onto cake to within 1 inch of edges. Sprinkle with pecans. Reroll cake without towel. Wrap in foil and freeze for at least 4 hours.

5 To serve, if desired, drizzle Raspberry Sauce over serving plates. Slice cake; place slices on plates. If desired, garnish with raspberries and mint.

NUTRITION FACTS PER SERVING: 182 calories, 4 g total fat (1 g saturated fat), 71 mg cholesterol, 146 mg sodium, 33 g carbohydrate, 0 g fiber, 6 g protein.

Raspberry Sauce: In a small saucepan heat ⅔ cup seedless raspberry spreadable fruit, 1 tablespoon lemon juice, and ¼ teaspoon almond extract until spreadable fruit is melted. Cool slightly.

Mint-Chocolate Cream Puffs

THE PERFECT ENDING FOR ANY MEAL, THESE ENTICING PUFFS ARE A CALORIE BARGAIN WITH ONLY 126 CALORIES PER SERVING.

Nonstick cooking spray
½ cup water
2 tablespoons butter
½ cup all-purpose flour
2 eggs

1 4-serving-size package fat-free instant chocolate pudding mix or reduced-calorie regular chocolate pudding mix
⅛ teaspoon peppermint extract

1 cup sliced fresh strawberries
Powdered sugar (optional)

EXCHANGES: 1½ Starch, ½ Fat **Prep:** 25 minutes **Bake:** 30 minutes **Chill:** 1 hour **Makes:** 8 servings

1 Coat a baking sheet with nonstick cooking spray. Set aside.

2 In a small saucepan combine the water and butter. Bring to boiling. Add flour all at once, stirring vigorously. Cook and stir until mixture forms a ball that doesn't separate. Remove from heat. Cool for 5 minutes. Add eggs, one at a time, beating after each addition until mixture is shiny and smooth. Drop mixture in 8 mounds 3 inches apart on the prepared baking sheet.

3 Bake in a 400° oven about 30 minutes or until golden brown. Remove from oven. Split puffs and remove any soft dough from inside. Cool completely on a wire rack.

4 Meanwhile, for filling, prepare pudding mix according to package directions. Stir in peppermint extract. Cover surface with plastic wrap. Chill in refrigerator 1 to 2 hours or until thoroughly chilled.

5 To serve, spoon about ¼ cup of the filling into the bottom half of each cream puff. Top with sliced strawberries. Replace tops. If desired, sprinkle with powdered sugar.

NUTRITION FACTS PER SERVING: 126 calories, 4 g total fat (2 g saturated fat), 61 mg cholesterol, 225 mg sodium, 20 g carbohydrate, 1 g fiber, 2 g protein.

Lemon Bars with Raspberries

YOUR GUESTS WILL NEVER GUESS HOW SIMPLE THESE IMPRESSIVE BARS ARE TO MAKE.

Nonstick cooking spray	**2** tablespoons all-purpose flour	**1½** cups fresh raspberries
¾ cup all-purpose flour	**1** teaspoon finely shredded lemon peel (set aside)	**2** tablespoons red currant jelly, melted
3 tablespoons sugar	**2** tablespoons lemon juice	
¼ cup butter	**1** tablespoon water	
1 egg	¼ teaspoon baking powder	
1 egg white		
⅔ cup sugar		

EXCHANGES: 1 Starch, ¹/₂ Fat **Prep:** 25 minutes
Bake: 15 minutes + 20 minutes **Cool:** 1 hour **Makes:** 18 triangles

1 Coat an 8×8×2-inch baking pan with nonstick cooking spray. Set aside. In a small bowl combine the ³/₄ cup flour and the 3 tablespoons sugar. Cut in butter until crumbly. Pat mixture onto the bottom of the pan. Bake in a 350° oven for 15 minutes.

2 For filling, in a small bowl combine egg and egg white. Beat with an electric mixer on medium speed until frothy. Add the ²/₃ cup sugar, the 2 tablespoons flour, the lemon juice, the water, and baking powder. Beat on medium speed about 3 minutes or until slightly thickened. Stir in lemon peel. Pour over hot baked layer in pan. Bake for 20 to 25 minutes more or until edges are light brown and center is set. Cool completely in pan on a wire rack. Cut into 9 squares; cut each square diagonally to make 2 triangles. Top triangles with raspberries. Drizzle with the jelly.

NUTRITION FACTS PER TRIANGLE: 96 calories, 3 g total fat (2 g saturated fat), 19 mg cholesterol, 40 mg sodium, 16 g carbohydrate, 1 g fiber, 1 g protein.

Autumn Apple Fritters

LEAVING THE PEEL ON THE APPLE RINGS SAVES TIME.

2 medium tart cooking apples (such as Jonathan or Granny Smith)	**¼** teaspoon baking powder
⅔ cup all-purpose flour	**1** egg
1 tablespoon powdered sugar	**½** cup fat-free milk
½ teaspoon finely shredded lemon peel	**1** teaspoon cooking oil
	Shortening or cooking oil for deep-fat frying
	Powdered sugar (optional)

EXCHANGES: ¹/₂ Fruit, 1¹/₂ Fat **Start to Finish:** 20 minutes **Makes:** 12 fritters

1 Core apples and cut each crosswise into 6 rings. In a medium bowl combine flour, the 1 tablespoon powdered sugar, the lemon peel, and baking powder.

2 In a bowl use a wire whisk to combine egg, milk, and the 1 teaspoon cooking oil. Add egg mixture all at once to flour mixture; beat until smooth.

3 Using a fork, dip apple rings into batter; drain off excess batter. Fry fritters, 2 or 3 at a time, in deep hot fat (365°) about 2 minutes or until golden, turning once with a slotted spoon. Drain on paper towels. If desired, sprinkle fritters with powdered sugar. Cool on wire racks.

NUTRITION FACTS PER FRITTER: 102 calories, 7 g total fat (1 g saturated fat), 18 mg cholesterol, 19 mg sodium, 9 g carbohydrate, 1 g fiber, 2 g protein.

Index

V-Z

Nutrition Facts: How They're Calculated

The following criteria were used to calculate the nutrition facts given with each recipe in this book:

- Optional ingredients were omitted.
- When ingredient options are given (for example: ground beef or ground pork), the nutrition facts were calculated using the first option.
- Unless another type of milk is specifically listed, 2% reduced-fat milk was used in the calculations.
- If a range of servings is given, the nutrition facts were based on the lowest number of servings listed.

Exchange Lists

FOLLOWING A HEALTHFUL MEAL PLAN IS ESSENTIAL IN THE TREATMENT OF DIABETES. THE EXCHANGE LISTS FOR MEAL PLANNING DEVELOPED BY THE AMERICAN DIABETES ASSOCIATION AND THE AMERICAN DIETETIC ASSOCIATION WILL MAKE THE JOB EASIER.

Counting exchanges is a shorthand technique for monitoring your food intake, especially carbohydrates. Before you begin using the exchange system, visit with your doctor and a registered dietitian. Together you can determine your calorie needs and come up with a daily meal plan based on your height, weight, activity level, lifestyle, and other health factors. The meal plan will tell you the number of servings from each food list that you are allowed per meal. Your dietitian also can give you some pointers for using exchanges successfully. After you've followed the plan for a while, you'll be able to judge if it fits your needs. If you find your plan is difficult to follow (for example, it includes more milk than you usually drink), ask your dietitian to help you make some alterations in the plan.

On the next few pages, you'll find charts that list the serving sizes for various foods. The lists are organized into Starch, Fruit, Milk, Other Carbohydrates, Vegetables, Meat and Meat Substitutes, Fat, Combination Foods, Fast Foods, and Free Foods.

Starch List

Bread/Count as 1 Starch Exchange

Bagel	½ (1 oz.)
Bread, reduced-calorie	2 slices (1½ oz.)
Bread (pumpernickel, rye, white, whole wheat)	1 slice (1 oz.)
Breadsticks, crisp, 4 x ½ inches	2 (⅔ oz.)
English muffin	½
Hot dog or hamburger bun	½ (1 oz.)
Pita, 6 inches across	½
Raisin bread, unfrosted	1 slice (1 oz.)
Roll, plain, small	1 (1 oz.)
Tortilla (corn), 6 inches across	1
Tortilla (flour), 7–8 inches across	1
Waffle, 4½-inch square, reduced-fat	1

Cereals and Grains/Count as 1 Starch Exchange

Bran cereals	½ cup
Bulgur	½ cup
Cereals, sugar-frosted	½ cup
Cereals, unsweetened, ready-to-eat	¾ cup
Cornmeal (dry)	3 Tbsp.
Couscous	⅓ cup
Flour (dry)	3 Tbsp.
Granola, low-fat	¼ cup
Grape Nuts	¼ cup
Grits	½ cup
Kasha	½ cup
Millet	¼ cup
Muesli	¼ cup
Oats	½ cup
Pasta	½ cup
Puffed cereal	1½ cups
Rice (brown or white)	⅓ cup
Rice milk	½ cup
Shredded wheat	½ cup
Wheat germ	3 Tbsp.

Crackers and Snacks/Count as 1 Starch Exchange

Animal crackers	8
Graham crackers, 2½-inch square	3
Matzoh	¾ oz.
Melba toast	4 slices
Oyster crackers	24
Popcorn (popped, no fat added or low-fat microwave)	3 cups
Pretzels	¾ oz.
Rice cakes, 4 inches across	2
Saltine-type crackers	6
Snack chips, fat-free (potato, tortilla)	15–20 (¾ oz.)
Whole wheat crackers, no fat added	2–5 (¾ oz.)

Starchy Vegetables/Count as 1 Starch Exchange

Baked beans	⅓ cup
Corn	½ cup
Corn on cob, medium	1 (5 oz.)
Mixed vegetables with corn, peas, or pasta	1 cup
Peas, green	½ cup
Plantain	½ cup
Potato, baked or boiled	1 small (3 oz.)
Potato, mashed	½ cup
Squash, winter (acorn, butternut)	1 cup
Yam, sweet potato, plain	½ cup

Dried Beans, Peas, and Lentils
Count as 1 Starch Exchange, plus 1
Very Lean Meat Exchange

Beans and peas (black-eyed, chickpea, kidney, pinto, split, white)	½ cup
Lentils	½ cup
Lima beans	⅔ cup

Starchy Foods Prepared with Fat
Count as 1 Starch Exchange, plus 1 Fat Exchange

Biscuit, 2½ inches across	1
Chow mein noodles	½ cup
Corn bread, 2-inch cube	1 (2 oz.)
Crackers, round butter type	6
Croutons	1 cup
French-fried potatoes	16 to 25 (3 oz.)
Granola	¼ cup
Muffin, small	1 (1½ oz.)
Pancake, 4 inches across	2
Popcorn, microwave	3 cups
Sandwich crackers (cheese or peanut butter filling)	3
Stuffing, bread, prepared	⅓ cup
Taco shell, 6 inches across	2
Waffle, 4½-inch square	1
Whole wheat crackers, fat added	4 to 6 (1 oz.)

Some foods purchased uncooked will weigh less after they are cooked. Starches often swell in cooking so a small amount of uncooked starch will become a much larger amount of cooked food. The following table shows these changes.

Food (Starch Group)	Uncooked	Cooked
Cream of Wheat	2 Tbsp.	½ cup
Dried beans	¼ cup	½ cup
Dried peas	¼ cup	½ cup
Grits	3 Tbsp.	½ cup
Lentils	3 Tbsp.	½ cup
Macaroni	¼ cup	½ cup
Noodles	⅓ cup	½ cup
Oatmeal	3 Tbsp.	½ cup
Rice	2 Tbsp.	⅓ cup
Spaghetti	¼ cup	½ cup

Fruit List

Fruit/Count as 1 Fruit Exchange

Apple, small, unpeeled	1 (4 oz.)
Apples, dried	4 rings
Applesauce, unsweetened	½ cup
Apricots, canned	½ cup
Apricots, dried	8 halves
Apricots, fresh	4 whole (5½ oz.)
Banana, small	1 (4 oz.)
Blackberries	¾ cup
Blueberries	¾ cup
Cantaloupe, small	⅓ melon (11 oz.) or 1 cup cubes
Cherries, sweet, canned	½ cup
Cherries, sweet, fresh	12 (3 oz.)
Dates	3
Figs, dried	1½
Figs, fresh	1½ large or 2 medium (3½ oz.)
Fruit cocktail	½ cup
Grapefruit, large	½ (11 oz.)
Grapefruit sections, canned	¾ cup
Grapes, small	17 (3 oz.)
Honeydew melon	1 slice (10 oz.) or 1 cup cubes
Kiwi fruit	1 (3½ oz.)
Mandarin oranges, canned	¾ cup
Mango, small	½ fruit (5½ oz.) or ½ cup
Nectarine, small	1 (5 oz.)
Orange, small	1 (6½ oz.)
Papaya	½ fruit (8 oz.) or 1 cup cubes
Peach, medium, fresh	1 (6 oz.)
Peaches, canned	½ cup
Pear, large, fresh	½ (4 oz.)
Pears, canned	½ cup
Pineapple, canned	½ cup
Pineapple, fresh	¾ cup
Plums, canned	½ cup
Plums, small	2 (5 oz.)
Prunes, dried	3
Raisins	2 Tbsp.
Raspberries	1 cup
Strawberries	1¼ cup whole berries
Tangerines, small	2 (8 oz.)
Watermelon	1 slice (13½ oz.) or 1¼ cup cubes

Fruit Juice/Count as 1 Fruit Exchange

Apple juice/cider	½ cup
Cranberry juice cocktail	⅓ cup
Cranberry juice cocktail, reduced-calorie	1 cup
Fruit juice blends, 100% juice	⅓ cup
Grapefruit juice	½ cup
Grape juice	⅓ cup
Orange juice	½ cup
Pineapple juice	½ cup
Prune juice	⅓ cup

Milk List

Fat-Free & Low-Fat Milk (0-3 g fat/serving)
Count as 1 Milk Exchange

Fat-free milk	1 cup
½% milk	1 cup
1% milk	1 cup
Fat-free or low-fat buttermilk	1 cup
Evaporated fat-free milk	½ cup
Fat-free dry milk	⅓ cup dry
Plain nonfat yogurt	¾ cup
Nonfat or low-fat fruit-flavored yogurt sweetened with aspartame or with a non-nutritive sweetener	1 cup

Reduced-Fat (5 g fat/serving)
Count as 1 Milk Exchange

2% milk	1 cup
Plain low-fat yogurt	¾ cup
Sweet acidophilus milk	1 cup

Whole Milk (8 g fat/serving)
Count as 1 Milk Exchange

Evaporated whole milk	½ cup
Goat's milk	1 cup
Whole milk	1 cup

Other Carbohydrates List

One Exchange equals 15 grams carbohydrate,
or 1 starch, or 1 fruit, or 1 milk.

Food/Count as 1 Carbohydrate Exchange	Serving Size	Exchanges Per Serving
Angel food cake, unfrosted	1/12 cake	2 carbohydrate
Brownie, small, unfrosted	2 in. square	1 carbohydrate, 1 fat
Cake, unfrosted	2 in. square	1 carbohydrate, 1 fat
Cake, frosted	2 in. square	2 carbohydrate, 1 fat
Chocolate milk, whole	1 cup	2 carbohydrate, 1 fat
Cookie, fat-free	2 small	1 carbohydrate
Cookie or sandwich cookie with creme filling	2 small	1 carbohydrate, 1 fat
Cranberry sauce, jellied	1/4 cup	2 carbohydrate
Cupcake, frosted	1 small	2 carbohydrate, 1 fat
Doughnut, plain cake	1 medium (1 1/2 oz)	1 1/2 carbohydrate, 2 fat
Doughnut, glazed	3 3/4 in. across (2 oz.)	2 carbohydrate, 2 fat
Fruit juice bars, frozen, 100% juice	1 bar (3 oz.)	1 carbohydrate
Fruit snacks, chewy (pureed fruit concentrate)	1 Tbsp.	1 carbohydrate
Fruit spreads, 100% fruit	1 Tbsp.	1 carbohydrate
Gelatin, regular	1/2 cup	1 carbohydrate
Gingersnaps	3	1 carbohydrate
Granola bar	1 bar	1 carbohydrate, 1 fat
Granola bar, fat-free	1 bar	2 carbohydrate
Honey	1 Tbsp.	1 carbohydrate
Hummus	1/3 cup	1 carbohydrate, 1 fat
Ice cream	1/2 cup	1 carbohydrate, 2 fat
Ice cream, light	1/2 cup	1 carbohydrate, 1 fat
Ice cream, fat-free, no sugar added	1/2 cup	1 carbohydrate
Jam or jelly, regular	1 Tbsp.	1 carbohydrate
Pie, fruit, 2 crusts	1/6 pie	3 carbohydrate, 2 fat
Pie pumpkin or custard	1/8 pie	1 carbohydrate, 2 fat
Potato chips	12-18 (1 oz.)	1 carbohydrate, 2 fat
Pudding, regular (made with low-fat milk)	1/2 cup	2 carbohydrate
Pudding, sugar-free (made with low-fat milk)	1/2 cup	1 carbohydrate
Salad dressing, fat-free*	1/4 cup	1 carbohydrate
Sherbet, sorbet	1/2 cup	2 carbohydrate
Spaghetti or pasta sauce, canned*	1/2 cup	1 carbohydrate, 1 fat
Sugar	1 Tbsp.	1 carbohydrate
Sweet roll or Danish	1 (2 1/2 oz.)	2 1/2 carbohydrate, 2 fat
Syrup, light	2 Tbsp.	1 carbohydrate
Syrup, regular	1 Tbsp.	1 carbohydrate
Syrup, regular	1/4 cup	4 carbohydrate
Tortilla chips	6-12 (1 oz.)	1 carbohydrate, 2 fat
Vanilla wafers	5	1 carbohydrate, 1 fat
Yogurt, frozen, low-fat, fat-free	1/3 cup	1 carbohydrate, 0-1 fat
Yogurt, frozen, fat-free, no sugar added	1/2 cup	1 carbohydrate
Yogurt, low-fat with fruit	1 cup	3 carbohydrate, 0-1 fat

*400 mg or more sodium per exchange

Vegetables List

Food	Uncooked	Cooked or Juice
Artichoke	1 cup	½ cup
Artichoke hearts	1 cup	½ cup
Asparagus	1 cup	½ cup
Beans (green, wax)	1 cup	½ cup
Bean sprouts	1 cup	½ cup
Beets	1 cup	½ cup
Broccoli	1 cup	½ cup
Brussels sprouts	1 cup	½ cup
Cabbage	1 cup	½ cup
Carrots	1 cup	½ cup
Cauliflower	1 cup	½ cup
Celery	1 cup	½ cup
Cucumber	1 cup	½ cup
Eggplant	1 cup	½ cup
Green onion/scallions	1 cup	½ cup
Greens (collard, kale, mustard, turnip)	1 cup	½ cup
Kohlrabi	1 cup	½ cup
Leeks	1 cup	½ cup
Mixed vegetables (no corn, peas, or pasta)	1 cup	½ cup

Food	Uncooked	Cooked or Juice
Mushrooms	1 cup	½ cup
Okra	1 cup	½ cup
Onions	1 cup	½ cup
Pea pods	1 cup	½ cup
Peppers (all varieties)	1 cup	½ cup
Radishes	1 cup	½ cup
Salad greens (endive, escarole, lettuce, romaine)	1 cup	½ cup
Sauerkraut*	1 cup	½ cup
Spinach	1 cup	½ cup
Summer squash	1 cup	½ cup
Tomato	1 cup	½ cup
Tomatoes, canned	1 cup	½ cup
Tomato sauce*	1 cup	½ cup
Tomato/vegetable juice*	1 cup	½ cup
Turnips	1 cup	½ cup
Water chestnuts	1 cup	½ cup
Watercress	1 cup	½ cup
Zucchini	1 cup	½ cup

*400 mg or more sodium per exchange

Meat & Meat Substitutes List

Very Lean Meat and Substitutes

One exchange equals 0 grams carbohydrate, 7 grams protein, 0 to 1 grams fat, and 35 calories.

Count as 1 Very Lean Meat Exchange

Fat-free cheese (≤1g fat/oz.)	1 oz.
Nonfat or low-fat cottage cheese (≤1g fat/oz.)	¼ cup
Fresh or frozen cod, flounder, haddock, halibut, trout, tuna (fresh or canned in water)	1 oz.
Buffalo, duck, or pheasant (no skin), ostrich, venison	1 oz.
Chicken or turkey (white meat, no skin), Cornish hen (no skin)	1 oz.
Clams, crab, imitation shellfish, lobster, scallops, shrimp	1 oz.
Egg substitutes, plain	¼ cup
Egg whites	2
Hot dogs with ≤ 1 g fat per ounce*	1 oz.
Kidney (high in cholesterol)	1 oz.
Processed sandwich meats with 1 gram or less fat per ounce such as chipped beef*, deli thin shaved meats, turkey ham	1 oz.
Sausage with ≤ 1g fat per ounce	1 oz.

Count as 1 Very Lean Meat Exchange and 1 Starch Exchange

Dried beans, lentils, peas (cooked)	½ cup

Lean Meat and Substitutes

One exchange equals 0 grams carbohydrate, 7 grams protein, 3 grams fat, and 55 calories.

Count as 1 Lean Meat Exchange

USDA Select or Choice grades of lean beef trimmed of fat, such as flank, round, and sirloin steak; ground round; roast (chuck, rib, rump); steak (cubed, porterhouse, T-bone); tenderloin	1 oz.
Cheeses (≤3g fat/oz.)	1 oz.
Chicken and turkey (dark meat, no skin), chicken white meat (with skin), domestic duck or goose (well-drained of fat, no skin)	1 oz.
Cottage cheese (4.5% fat)	¼ cup
Game: Goose (no skin), rabbit	1 oz.
Herring (uncreamed or smoked)	1 oz.
Hot dogs (≤3g fat/oz.*)	1½ oz.
Lamb: Chop, leg, roast	1 oz.
Liver, heart (high in cholesterol)	1 oz.
Oysters	6 medium
Parmesan, grated	2 Tbsp.
Pork (lean), such as boiled, canned, or cured ham; Canadian-style bacon*; center loin chop; fresh ham; tenderloin	1 oz.
Processed sandwich meat with (≤3g fat/oz.) such as kielbasa or turkey pastrami	1 oz.
Salmon (fresh or canned), catfish	1 oz.
Sardines (canned)	2 medium
Tuna (canned in oil, drained)	1 oz.
Veal, lean chop, roast	1 oz.

*400 mg or more sodium per exchange

Medium-Fat Meat and Substitutes

One exchange equals 0 grams carbohydrate,
7 grams protein, 5 grams fat, and 75 calories.

Count as 1 Medium-Fat Meat Exchange

Most beef products fall into this category (corned beef; ground beef; meat loaf; Prime grades of meat trimmed of fat, such as prime rib; short ribs)	1 oz.
Chicken dark meat (with skin), fried chicken (with skin), ground turkey or ground chicken	1 oz.
Egg (high in cholesterol, limit to 3 per week)	1
Feta cheese (≤5g fat/oz.)	1 oz.
Fish (any fried fish product)	1 oz.
Lamb (ground, rib roast)	1 oz.
Mozzarella cheese (≤5g fat/oz.)	1 oz.
Pork (Boston butt, chop, cutlet, top loin)	1 oz.
Ricotta cheese (≤5g fat/oz.)	2 oz. (¼ cup)
Sausage (≤5g fat/oz.)	1 oz.
Soy milk	1 cup
Tofu	4 oz. (½ cup)
Veal cutlet (cubed or ground, unbreaded)	1 oz.

High-Fat Meat and Substitutes

One exchange equals 0 grams carbohydrate,
7 grams protein, 8 grams fat, and 100 calories.

These items are high in saturated fat, cholesterol, and calories and may raise blood cholesterol levels if eaten regularly.

Count as 1 High-Fat Meat Exchange

Bacon	3 slices (20 slices/lb.)
Cheese (all regular cheeses, such as American*, cheddar, Monterey Jack, Swiss)	1 oz.
Hot dog (chicken or turkey)*	1 (10/lb.)
Pork (ground pork, pork sausage, spareribs)	1 oz.
Processed sandwich meat such as bologna, pimiento loaf, salami (≤5g fat/oz.)	1 oz.
Sausage, such as bratwurst, Italian, knockwurst, Polish, smoked	1 oz.

Count as 1 High-Fat Meat plus 1 Fat Exchange

Hot dog (beef, pork, or combination)*	1 (10/lb.)
Peanut butter (contains unsaturated fat)	2 Tbsp.

*400 mg or more sodium per exchange

Fat List

One Fat Exchange equals 5 grams fat and 45 calories.

Monounsaturated Fats List/Count as 1 Fat Exchange

Almonds, cashews	6 nuts
Avocado, medium	⅛ (1 oz.)
Green olives, stuffed*	10 large
Mixed nuts (50% peanuts)	6 nuts
Oil (canola, olive, peanut)	1 tsp.
Peanut butter, smooth or crunchy	2 tsp.
Peanuts	10 nuts
Pecans	4 halves
Ripe (black) olives	8 large
Sesame seeds	1 Tbsp.
Tahini paste	2 tsp.

Polyunsaturated Fats List/Count as 1 Fat Exchange

Margarine lower-fat (30% to 50% vegetable oil)	1 Tbsp.
Margarine stick, tub, or squeeze	1 tsp.
Mayonnaise (reduced-fat)	1 Tbsp.
Mayonnaise (regular)	1 tsp.
Miracle Whip Salad Dressing (reduced fat)	1 Tbsp.
Miracle Whip Salad Dressing (regular)	2 tsp.

Oil (corn, safflower, soybean)	1 tsp.
Salad dressing (reduced-fat)	2 Tbsp.
Salad dressing (regular)*	1 Tbsp.
Seeds (pumpkin, sunflower)	1 Tbsp.
Walnuts	4 halves

Saturated Fats List/Count as 1 Fat Exchange

Bacon, cooked	1 slice (20 slices/lb.)
Bacon grease	1 tsp.
Butter (reduced-fat)	1 Tbsp.
Butter (stick)	1 tsp.
Butter (whipped)	2 tsp.
Coconut, sweetened, shredded	2 Tbsp.
Cream, half-and-half	2 Tbsp.
Cream cheese (reduced-fat)	2 Tbsp. (1 oz.)
Cream cheese (regular)	1 Tbsp. (½ oz.)
Shortening or lard	1 tsp.
Sour cream (reduced-fat)	3 Tbsp.
Sour cream (regular)	2 Tbsp.

*400 mg or more sodium per exchange
**Saturated fats can raise blood cholesterol levels if eaten regularly.

Combination Foods List

Entrées/Count as 1 Combination Food Exchange	Serving Size	Exchanges Per Serving
Tuna noodle casserole, chili with beans, lasagna, macaroni and cheese, spaghetti with meatballs*	1 cup (8 oz.)	2 carbohydrate, 2 medium-fat meat
Chow mein (without noodles or rice)*	2 cups (16 oz.)	1 carbohydrate, 2 lean meat
Pizza, cheese, thin crust*	¼ of 10 in. (5 oz.)	2 carbohydrate, 2 medium-fat meat, 1 fat
Pizza, meat topping, thin crust*	¼ of 10 in. (5 oz.)	2 carbohydrate, 2 medium-fat meat, 2 fat
Potpie*	1 (7 oz.)	2 carbohydrate, 1 medium-fat meat, 4 fat

Frozen entrées/Count as 1 Combination Food Exchange	Serving Size	Exchanges Per Serving
Entrée with less than 300 calories	1 (8 oz.)	2 carbohydrate, 3 lean meat
Salisbury steak with gravy, mashed potato*	1 (11 oz.)	2 carbohydrate, 3 medium-fat meat, 3-4 fat
Turkey with gravy, mashed potato, dressing*	1 (11 oz.)	2 carbohydrate, 2 medium-fat meat, 2 fat

Soup/Count as 1 Combination Food Exchange	Serving Size	Exchanges Per Serving
Bean*	1 cup (8 oz.)	1 carbohydrate, 1 very lean meat
Cream (made with water)*	1 cup (8 oz.)	1 carbohydrate, 1 fat
Split pea (made with water)*	½ cup (4 oz.)	1 carbohydrate
Tomato (made with water)*	1 cup (8 oz.)	1 carbohydrate
Vegetable beef, chicken noodle, or other broth-type*	1 cup (8 oz.)	1 carbohydrate

Fast Foods

Food	Serving Size	Exchanges Per Serving
Burritos with beef*	2	4 carbohydrate, 2 medium-fat meat, 2 fat
Chicken nuggets*	6	1 carbohydrate, 2 medium-fat meat, 1 fat
Chicken breast and wing, breaded and fried*	1 each	1 carbohydrate, 4 medium-fat meat, 2 fat
Fish sandwich with tartar sauce*	1	3 carbohydrate, 1 medium-fat meat, 3 fat
French fries, thin*	20-25	2 carbohydrate, 2 fat
Hamburger, regular	1	2 carbohydrate, 2 medium-fat meat
Hamburger, large*	1	2 carbohydrate, 3 medium-fat meat, 1 fat
Hot dog with bun*	1	1 carbohydrate, 1 high-fat meat, 1 fat
Individual pan pizza*	1	5 carbohydrate, 3 medium-fat meat, 3 fat
Soft-serve cone	1 medium	2 carbohydrate, 1 fat
Submarine sandwich*	1 sub (6 in.)	3 carbohydrate, 1 vegetable, 2 medium-fat meat, 1 fat
Taco, hard shell*	1 (6 oz.)	2 carbohydrate, 2 medium-fat meat, 2 fat
Taco, soft shell*	1 (3 oz.)	1 carbohydrate, 1 medium-fat meat, 1 fat

*400 mg or more sodium per exchange

Free Foods List

A free food is any food or drink that contains less than 5 grams carbohydrate and less than 20 calories per serving.

Fat-Free or Reduced-Fat Foods

Cream cheese, fat-free	1 Tbsp.
Creamers, nondairy, liquid	1 Tbsp.
Creamers, nondairy, powdered	2 tsp.
Margarine, fat-free	4 Tbsp.
Margarine, reduced-fat	1 tsp.
Mayonnaise, fat-free	1 Tbsp.
Mayonnaise, reduced-fat	1 tsp.
Miracle Whip, nonfat	1 Tbsp.
Miracle Whip, reduced-fat	1 tsp.
Nonstick cooking spray	
Salad dressing, fat-free	1 Tbsp.
Salad dressing, fat-free, Italian	2 Tbsp.
Salsa	¼ cup
Sour cream, fat-free, reduced-fat	1 Tbsp.
Whipped topping, regular or light	2 Tbsp.

Sugar-Free or Low-Sugar Foods

Candy, hard, sugar-free	1 candy
Gelatin, unflavored	
Gelatin dessert, sugar-free	
Gum, sugar-free	
Jam or jelly, low-sugar or light	2 tsp.
Sugar substitutes†	
Syrup, sugar-free	2 Tbsp.

†Sugar substitutes, alternatives, or replacements that are approved by the Food and Drug Administration (FDA) are considered to be safe to use. Common brand names include: Equal (aspartame), Splenda (sucralose), Sprinkle Sweet (saccharin), Sugar Twin (saccharin), Sweet 'n' Low (saccharin), Sweet One (acesulfame K), Sweet-10 (saccharin).

Drinks

Bouillon, broth, consommé*	
Carbonated or mineral water	
Club soda or tonic water, sugar-free	
Cocoa powder, unsweetened	1 Tbsp.
Coffee and tea	
Diet soft drinks, sugar-free	
Drink mixes, sugar-free	

Condiments

Catsup	1 Tbsp.
Horseradish	
Lemon or lime juice	
Mustard	
Pickles, dill*	1½ large
Soy sauce, regular or light*	
Taco sauce	1 Tbsp.
Vinegar	

Seasonings**

Flavoring extracts
Garlic
Herbs, fresh or dried
Pimiento
Spices
Tabasco or hot pepper sauce
Wine, used in cooking
Worcestershire sauce

*400 mg or more sodium per exchange

**Use seasonings sparingly that contain sodium or seasonings that are salts, such as garlic or celery salt and lemon pepper.

Metric Information

The charts on this page provide a guide for converting measurements from the U.S. customary system, which is used throughout this book, to the metric system.

Product Differences

Most of the ingredients called for in the recipes in this book are available in most countries. However, some are known by different names. Here are some common American ingredients and their possible counterparts:

- Sugar (white) is granulated, fine granulated, or castor sugar.
- Powdered sugar is icing sugar.
- All-purpose flour is enriched, bleached or unbleached white household flour. When self-rising flour is used in place of all-purpose flour in a recipe that calls for leavening, omit the leavening agent (baking soda or baking powder) and salt.
- Light-colored corn syrup is golden syrup.
- Cornstarch is cornflour.
- Baking soda is bicarbonate of soda.
- Vanilla or vanilla extract is vanilla essence.
- Green, red, or yellow sweet peppers are capsicums or bell peppers.
- Golden raisins are sultanas.

Volume and Weight

The United States traditionally uses cup measures for liquid and solid ingredients. The chart below shows the approximate imperial and metric equivalents. If you are accustomed to weighing solid ingredients, the following approximate equivalents will be helpful.

- 1 cup butter, castor sugar, or rice = 8 ounces = $1/2$ pound = 250 grams
- 1 cup flour = 4 ounces = $1/4$ pound = 125 grams
- 1 cup icing sugar = 5 ounces = 150 grams

Canadian and U.S. volume for a cup measure is 8 fluid ounces (237 ml), but the standard metric equivalent is 250 ml.

1 British imperial cup is 10 fluid ounces.

In Australia, 1 tablespoon equals 20 ml, and there are 4 teaspoons in the Australian tablespoon.

Spoon measures are used for smaller amounts of ingredients. Although the size of the tablespoon varies slightly in different countries, for practical purposes and for recipes in this book, a straight substitution is all that's necessary. Measurements made using cups or spoons always should be level unless stated otherwise.

Common Weight Range Replacements

Imperial / U.S.	Metric
½ ounce	15 g
1 ounce	25 g or 30 g
4 ounces (¼ pound)	115 g or 125 g
8 ounces (½ pound)	225 g or 250 g
16 ounces (1 pound)	450 g or 500 g
1¼ pounds	625 g
1½ pounds	750 g
2 pounds or 2¼ pounds	1,000 g or 1 Kg

Oven Temperature Equivalents

Fahrenheit Setting	Celsius Setting*	Gas Setting
300°F	150°C	Gas Mark 2 (very low)
325°F	160°C	Gas Mark 3 (low)
350°F	180°C	Gas Mark 4 (moderate)
375°F	190°C	Gas Mark 5 (moderate)
400°F	200°C	Gas Mark 6 (hot)
425°F	220°C	Gas Mark 7 (hot)
450°F	230°C	Gas Mark 8 (very hot)
475°F	240°C	Gas Mark 9 (very hot)
500°F	260°C	Gas Mark 10 (extremely hot)
Broil	Broil	Grill

*Electric and gas ovens may be calibrated using celsius. However, for an electric oven, increase celsius setting 10 to 20 degrees when cooking above 160°C. For convection or forced air ovens (gas or electric), lower the temperature setting 25°F/10°C when cooking at all heat levels.

Baking Pan Sizes

Imperial / U.S.	Metric
9×1½-inch round cake pan	22- or 23×4-cm (1.5 L)
9×1½-inch pie plate	22- or 23×4-cm (1 L)
8×8×2-inch square cake pan	20×5-cm (2 L)
9×9×2-inch square cake pan	22- or 23×4.5-cm (2.5 L)
11×7×1½-inch baking pan	28×17×4-cm (2 L)
2-quart rectangular baking pan	30×19×4.5-cm (3 L)
13×9×2-inch baking pan	34×22×4.5-cm (3.5 L)
15×10×1-inch jelly roll pan	40×25×2-cm
9×5×3-inch loaf pan	23×13×8-cm (2 L)
2-quart casserole	2 L

U.S. / Standard Metric Equivalents

⅛ teaspoon = 0.5 ml	
¼ teaspoon = 1 ml	
½ teaspoon = 2 ml	
1 teaspoon = 5 ml	
1 tablespoon = 15 ml	
2 tablespoons = 25 ml	
¼ cup = 2 fluid ounces = 50 ml	
⅓ cup = 3 fluid ounces = 75 ml	
½ cup = 4 fluid ounces = 125 ml	
⅔ cup = 5 fluid ounces = 150 ml	
¾ cup = 6 fluid ounces = 175 ml	
1 cup = 8 fluid ounces = 250 ml	
2 cups = 1 pint = 500 ml	
1 quart = 1 litre	